DIARY

OF

A SPECIAL MUM

Kicking Autism To The Curb

DELLY SINGAH

CORNERSTONE
PUBLISHING HOUSE

London

Scripture quotations taken from the Holy Bible, New International Version®, NIV®. Copyright © 1973, 1978, 1984, 2011 by Biblica, Inc.™ Used by permission of Zondervan. Scripture quotations taken from the Amplified Bible, Copyright © 1954, 1958, 1962, 1964, 1965, 1987 by The Lockman Foundation. Used by permission.

DIARY OF A SPECIAL MUM

British Library Cataloguing in Publication Data.

A CIP catalogue record for this book is available from the British Library

ISBN: 978-1-918040-00-5

Printed in the U.K.

First Printing 2025.
Ordering Information:
Quantity Sales: Special discounts are available on quantity purchases by corporations, associations, schools, seminaries and others. For details, contact the publisher.

CORNERSTONE
PUBLISHING HOUSE

London

DEDICATION

I dedicate this book to all parents raising autistic children. You are indeed the unsung heroes of our society.

> *"Autism is not a tragedy. It's a challenge that can be met with creativity, courage, and resolve."*
> **[Senator Tom Harkin, Autism Advocate]**

ACKNOWLEDGEMENTS

"Autism is a spectrum. This does not mean that everyone is a bit autistic. It means that every autistic person experiences different combinations of autistic traits and each to different intensities. It is non-linear and our ability to cope with different things varies day to day."

[Emily Katy]

My heartfelt appreciation goes to JB's Dad – Mr. Philip O. Samson, Stanley Nchitu – JB's Godfather, Dilys Singah – JB's favourite Aunty, JB's favourite Carer Yemi, Mary – the therapist, Mr. Abdi Hassan & Fatima – his Drivers and Vicky - his class Teacher.

The following leaders, uncles and aunties have made tremendous positive contributions to JB:

Rev. Jesse Song, Pastor Brenda A. Kimbu, Prof. Victor Mbarika, Mr. Oladeji BG, Mr. Simon Pekeleke, Mr. Anderson Aka Nkafu, Mr. Emmanuel Afa Siben, Mr. Henry Namputu, Mr. Patrice Tamo, Mr. Didier Dimala, Mr. Lavert Nchitu, Mr. Lesley Abei, Jayjay Bilika, Mr. Solomon Achankeng, Mr. Jude Adzeyuf.

Mummy Love Pekeleke, Mrs. Victorine Ndikum (Mummy Vicky),Ms. Ngwefah Akum Amang, Mrs. Lawrencia Kwanga, Ms. Nora Brown, Mrs. Naomi Edeme, Mrs. Lizette Forkwa

Bilika, Mrs. Sandy Sah Abah, Mrs. Linda Brown, Mrs. Debbie Semah, Mrs. Alice Oshogwe, Mrs. Nina Abei and Baby Aviel Abei.

Royal City Mission – London

Nexus Primary School – Tonbridge

Bexley Council – London

Evidently, it takes an entire community to raise a child. An even more intentional, dedicated, sacrificial and loving community to raise a special needs child.

TABLE OF CONTENTS

DEDICATION.. iii

ACKNOWLEDGEMENTS.. v

TABLE OF CONTENTS... vii

PREFACE... ix

FOREWORD.. xv

INTRODUCTION xix

CHAPTER 1
THE SPECTRUM...1

CHAPTER 2
BREAKING THE STEREOTYPES.....................................19

CHAPTER 3
EARLY AND LATER TRAITS..29

CHAPTER 4
STAGES OF GRIEF...49

CHAPTER 5
DO'S AND DON'TS...69

CHAPTER 6
CHALLENGES OF AUTISTIC PARENTS..........................87

CHAPTER 7
SIGNIFICANT PERSONS TO AUTISTIC CHILDREN.......105

CHAPTER 8
AUTISM – NUTRITION CONNECTION............................121

CHAPTER 9:
THE ADVENTURES OF JB...137

TESTIMONIALS...165

REFERENCES...173

> *"Autists are the ultimate square pegs, and the problem with pounding a square peg into a round hole is not that the hammering is hard work. It's that you're destroying the peg"*
>
> **[Paul Collins]**

PREFACE

My mind is a muse, an intricate dance
Of shapes, sounds, and sensations colliding.
Thoughts come together like fragments of glass,
Reflecting meanings, I often struggle to share.
I feel deeply—joy, pain, and everything in between—
But my face wears a mask,
Hiding the storms and whispers beneath.

I carry fears, perhaps too many,
And the world feels like it's always too loud,
Too bright, or too overwhelming.
Rain falls like a crashing storm,
Sunlight burns like a blazing fire,
And laughter shakes the ground beneath me.
These fears flow like a flood with no escape,
Trapping me within their rising tide.
I see your lips move, but your words slip past.
I hear the rhythm of your heart,

But it doesn't resonate with mine.

The music you play may sound beautiful,

But at times, my world is numb to its melody.

You may see me as something foreign,

A mystery, a curse, or a failure.

But I am none of those—I am human.

Different, yes, but difference is what makes life colorful.

A rainbow isn't whole if even one shade is lost.

I was born this way,

With a mind that perceives the world differently.

A spectrum of thoughts and emotions,

Complex and misunderstood.

Yet, my uniqueness isn't a flaw—it's a wonder,

A world within me that deserves to be known.

They call it Autism.

Mummy calls it love.

JB

My dearest Son,

Prior to meeting your father, I had seen you, I knew I was having a son as my first. Don't ask me how, I was so sure and I did! When I got married to your father, I couldn't wait to carry you, I did! Then I impatiently waited to hear you tell me you were there. You did, with your first kick, a second and countless more. I was happy and couldn't wait to hold you in my arms. I had plans for you, how I wanted life to be. I'd hoped you would become a model, so I made a collection of child models pictures I'd seen online. I was sure you'll rock those stylish little outfits better than them.

I was certain you'll turn out to be a good child. I planned on teaching you how to pray and have a personal relationship with God; hence I gave you the name "Jesus Boy". So now, each time you say "Amen" after every prayer, I feel so accomplished. I planned on teaching you everything worth learning. Little did I know you would be the one teaching me more of these things. Oops! Life doesn't always turn out as planned and God's will for us is ultimate.

You've shown me the true meaning of love - Agape Love. Even when I make you cry from shaving your hair, I'm still the first you run to as a shield. Even when you're overwhelmed by my excesses, all you do is put your fingers in your ears. It is how your face lights up each time you see me approaching the school bus, then the tight hugs I'll get from you thereafter. Nothing beats that!

I'd give anything to protect you from pain, but I've learned that my job isn't to shield you from every struggle. Instead, it's to walk beside you, to comfort you, and to help you rise stronger after every fall. You've taught me what patience really looks like. I used to rush through life, but you've shown me how small things like preparing you for school or just holding your little fingers while we walk down the street can transform difficult moments into easier ones. Your happiness makes every effort worthwhile.

You've helped me hear and see the world in new ways. While I once overlooked the finer details, you notice everything—the rhythm of a song from a distance, the grain of rice that drops from your plate when you eat, the beauty in your routines; the uniqueness in everything you do. You've taught me that being different isn't just okay—it's incredible! You've also taught me courage. Before you, I avoided conflict and tried to keep the peace. But for you, I've found a strength I didn't know I had. I'll fight for you, advocate for you, and push past any barrier to make sure you have every opportunity you deserve. You're worth it! Most importantly, you've taught me to embrace and celebrate what makes you unique. At first, I wanted so badly for you to fit in, to be like the other kids. I wanted you to love football and hoped you'll play for Chelsea FC someday. But no, you are afraid of the ball and wouldn't even come close to it. It is the many designer outfits I bought, yet you prefer one particular regular shirt, trousers and sneakers. Then I let you follow your passions—whether it is just watching your favourite cartoon - (the lion and the little bug), singing the wrong lyrics to your favourite songs, playing the drums in Church after service, or the small things that brought you joy like munching your favourite bag of potato crisps, forwarding and rewinding a video you find pleasure in or taking a thousand pictures of your flickering fingers with my phone.

I realised you weren't meant to blend in. You were meant to stand out. I'm sorry for the times I tried to make you fit into a world that wasn't built for you. You are exactly as you should be—brilliant, unique, perfect and a Jesus Boy. Thank you for being my teacher, my inspiration, and my greatest gift. You've made me a better person, and I am forever grateful.

Love you, always!
Mummy

"Autism is not a problem to be solved, but a reality to be experienced with joy."
[Gilles Trehin, Autism Advocate]

FOREWORD

It is not often that one finds a book that stirs the emotions and challenges the mind. Delly Singah has succeeded brilliantly in doing just that in *The Diary of a Special Mum* as she brings us into the world of autism.

The point is made poignantly clear through these pages that autism is not a condition to be feared—it is a reality to be understood. Yet, in many communities, particularly in Africa, autism remains shrouded in "misunderstanding, stigma, and silence" as Delly points out. This book is a loud and powerful response to that silence.

At its core, *Diary of a Special Mum* is a deeply personal yet universally relevant account of a mother's journey—a journey marked by "love, resilience, and an unwavering commitment to her son, JB". Her voice, raw and unfiltered, adds to the much-needed conversation on awareness, acceptance, and advocacy for children on the autism spectrum.

It may come to many as a surprise that autism is a spectrum; that no two individuals experience it the same

way. Yet, there are commonalities that unite the autistic –
"challenges in communication, sensory processing, and
social interaction" – but also unique strengths, abilities, and
perspectives that demand to be recognized and nurtured. The
book masterfully weaves together "scientific insights with
personal testimonies", offering both an "educational
resource and an emotional guide" for families, caregivers,
educators, and policymakers.

What makes this book particularly vital is its focus
on shifting "societal perspectives on autism in Africa". In a
region where developmental disorders are often
misunderstood or misdiagnosed, the need for awareness and
"a culture of tolerance, empathy, and zero discrimination"
cannot be overstated. By sharing her experience, the author
not only "breaks stereotypes but also transforms mindsets",
paving the way for a future where neurodiverse children are
embraced, supported, and empowered.

But this book is more than just one mother's story. It
is a "manual for change", a true "beacon of hope", and a "call
to action" for millions in Africa and beyond. It urges families
to seek understanding, educators to embrace inclusive
learning, and society at large to recognize that, as the author

puts it, "autism is not a limitation—it is a different way of experiencing the world".

As you turn these pages, I invite you to read with an open mind and heart. Whether you are a parent, a teacher, a policymaker, or simply someone seeking to understand autism better, this book will leave you "informed, inspired, and ready to be part of the change". Let us listen. Let us learn. Let us build a world where every child, regardless of where they fall on the spectrum, is seen, heard, and valued.

Delly Singah is a respected humanitarian, media personnel, advocate and author based in London, known for her firm stance and work in raising awareness about important social issues, including relationships, autism and neurodiversity, particularly within African communities. Through her writing, she challenges misconceptions, breaks societal stereotypes, and promotes inclusivity and understanding for individuals on the autism spectrum.

This book on autism, *Diary of a Special Mum*, is a deeply personal and insightful account of her journey as a mother navigating the challenges and triumphs of raising a child with autism. Beyond sharing her experience, she uses her platform to make the case for better support systems for neurodivergent children, ensuring they receive the acceptance, resources, and opportunities they deserve.

As a blogger and social commentator, Delly engages with a global audience, using digital platforms to spark conversations about parenting, mental health, and neurodiversity. Her work serves as an essential voice in reshaping perceptions of autism, particularly in African communities where awareness and resources remain limited.

Mr Eric Chinje

Director of Strategic Communications, Mo Ibrahim Foundation

Former Manager, Global Media Development, World Bank

INTRODUCTION

"It takes a village to raise a child. It takes a child with autism to raise the consciousness of the village."
[Coach Elaine Hall]

The World Health Organization (2022) estimates that autism affects 0.7–21.1 per 10,000 children globally. An approximately 6 out of every 10,000 children born in Cameroon are autistic. The U.N. (2013) estimated that 700,000 people in Cameroon have autism.

Characterised by delayed diagnosis, limited access to services, stigma and stereotypes. Just like many of you, I knew nothing about Autism until my son was almost two.

"Jesus Boy" (JB) as I fondly call my son was born at the Lewisham Teaching Hospital - London, 36 weeks prepartum, weighing 2.67kg. He came early as I had gestational diabetes; he was big and breached. So, I had to undergo a caesarean section (CS). It was successful and I don't know how to express the joy of hearing him cry the very first time. When JB was born, he was literally the most beautiful baby in the Hospital Ward - as was described by the Nurses. He was as coloured as a mixed-race child, big white eyes, curly hairs, cute fingers and toes. He was a charmer; very lively, playful and constantly smiling. He had the most beautiful smile I'd seen and he was quite generous with it, even to strangers. He was (still is) a sweet child and apart from his good looks, he had such a charming personality at his age. He'd smile at the bus driver, the lady at the groceries, the Teller at the bank, everyone in Church and of course, at me. He was always smiling. He would eat everything; chicken drumsticks were his favourite. I still remember watching him struggle with just two teeth biting chicken drumsticks, having gripped it so firmly you could barely take it away from him. He rejected breast milk and was immediately put-on formula. He ate every African food served to him even with mild chilli. JB was literally a foodie.

I had plans of doing dreadlocks on his hair and had already started doing so with the baby hairs pending when the hard ones would grow. He was very OK with me playing with his hair and wouldn't mind me touching for as long as I did. He was OK with every outfit and accessories I clad him in - hats, gloves, socks and jackets. As early as 12-18 months, he was already calling "daddy, bye, hello". I was excited and couldn't wait to hear him add "Mama" to his vocabulary. He was always chatty, bubbly, eager and so full of life! JB would speak to you and anyone by him. Muttering words and giggling as he did. Everyone adored him. He was OK going from hand to hand and everyone wanted to carry such a cute boy. He could barely walk. He crawled and was quite scared of standing. All was going on fine and it seemed like motherhood looked great on me. Then suddenly, everything took a downward spiral.

Autism is a spectrum; a very broad spectrum. Every special child is on a different one yet they all have common denominators (for the most part) they share. As a parent, I'd advise you to trust your mummy/daddy instinct(s). You'll hardly go wrong with it. You should know your child better than any other. Be vigilant from birth and monitor their growth; growth in all aspects. It becomes difficult to miss out on the slightest change that could happen. They have their world. You must get into this world of theirs to understand and better relate with them.

Why did I write this book?

Predominantly, for educational purposes. As a public figure, such sensitisations will cause more impact and possibly reach avenues where I can't be physically present. Joining my voice to create the much-needed awareness on Autism amongst (especially) my African community; breaking stereotypes, transforming mindsets and creating a culture of tolerance, empathy and zero discrimination. Some innocent children face devastating false accusations of witchcraft in certain places and families, often stemming from deeply rooted cultural beliefs, societal fears and gross ignorance on the subject. These children, sometimes as young as when the traits get obvious, are labelled all sorts of cruel adjectives leading to severe stigmatisation, abuse, and even abandonment. These accusations have been known to result in horrific consequences, including violence, ostracism and starvation. Some families become so embarrassed to the point of locking up these kids indoors and they are never seen anywhere amongst people.

Looking back, I was as ignorant and erroneous with my approach towards the spectrum. It's taken me having, living with and caring for an Autist to really comprehend their setup (still not entirely). Thankfully, more NGOs and local activists are raising awareness to protect these vulnerable children/persons; highlighting the urgent need for more education and sensitisation to break these stereotypes.

Away from the kids, equally pointing towards the ripple effect Autism has on marriages/divorces and the need to curb the excesses. Has it occurred to you the number of broken homes Autism has rendered, simply because Africans (especially) choose to rather be superstitious?

My journey as a Special Parent has been the most intriguing thing ever; a perfect blend of good days, bad days, mundane ones, loneliness, inadequacy, warm hugs, hysterical laughter, curiosity, learning and this diary. To every other Special Parent reading this, this is my love letter to you with a virtual hug herein. We are in this together!

Writing this book - sharing a huge part of my private life with the world in the most vulnerable way - has been the most emotional thing I have had to do. For JB, spreading love to his peers; is perhaps connected to his purpose on earth. This is a Diary - my Diary. It is a progressive narrative, requiring further write ups that will continue to equip us with the necessary tools to kick autism to the curb.

> *"Autism is not a disease. Don't try to cure us. Try to understand us."*
> **[Alexandra Forshaw, Autism Advocate]**

CHAPTER 1:

THE SPECTRUM

"Autism is seeing the world from a different perspective, yet appreciating the beauty in its uniqueness".
[Delly Singah]

When you hear of anything whose origin is unknown, it becomes frightening because the next phase of that thing could be anything. At that point, you are uncertain what to expect and how best to be positioned. Position for what exactly? Prepare for what? And how exactly? Worse still, the gross ignorance, the cold stigma, the alarming prevalence rate of one in every 160 children globally, diagnosed with autism spectrum disorder (World Health Organisation statistics). This is one child too many!

On 09 September 2019, my son - JB at 3 years and 4 months of age, was clinically diagnosed with Autism - characterised by severe speech and language difficulties, regression in mental development, severe social communication difficulties, mild motor skills difficulties. I'd initially raised concerns when he was 2 years and two months (rough estimation) and he was only first granted

1

access to a Community Paediatrics when he was 2 years and 8-10 months. Prior to this date, I had no idea what Autism was about. I only got to find out about the term on Google when researching on the traits I noticed from my son. I didn't quite understand what it meant. I became curious and started reading, researching and asking questions. The more I did, the more frightening it got. I recall booking an appointment with the Doctor just to tell him about some Autism I'd discovered and my hope was to get a more detailed explanation of what it is and of course, be prescribed a drug or two for my son. I was wrong and my hopes came crashing when I realised there was a chance, "this thing called autism" could potentially last a lifetime. The Mother in me immediately rejected it. (You can read more on this in chapter 4 on "Dealing with Grief").

According to the National Institute of Mental Health, "autism spectrum disorder (ASD) is a neurological and developmental disorder that affects how people interact with others, communicate, learn, and behave. Although autism can be diagnosed at any age, it is described as a "developmental disorder" because symptoms generally appear in the first 2 years of life." Breaking the above definition down, here's my understanding of what Autism means.

"Neurological", meaning, it has to do with the nervous system. This nervous system is made up of the brain, the spinal cord and the nerves. Meaning, it is how the entire body communicates with the brain and how the brain responds back to the body. The brain, through your nerves, powers the body's senses and helps them interpret what is being heard, felt, tasted and perceived in your environment. So, the brain tells the body how to think, what to understand, what to retain, how to feel and when to react.

Autism and Mutation (Caterpillar to Butterfly)

Understand I am not a medic, neither am I an expert. This is only a mother's attempt to understand the various transitions her son has gone through since birth as far as ASD is concerned. I believe the essence of education is in its simplification for comprehension. Hence, I break it down to the bare minimum and to the best of my understanding. Hopefully, I'm not wrong.

Autism spectrum disorder (ASD) is associated with rare mutations in many genes, including those that affect brain development. These mutations can be inherited from parents or occur spontaneously in eggs or sperm. These mutations are alterations or changes that happen in the DNA sequence of an organism without reverting to its original form. Mutations could either be by deletion, duplication,

3

inversion or translocation. Now, let me further break down the above grammar with the analogy of the caterpillar and butterfly. Though this process is more of Metamorphosis and the term mutation is not very appropriate, it however comes close to showcasing my understanding of what ASD means.

There are four stages in the life cycle of a butterfly - the egg, larva, pupa and adult. Metamorphosis happens when the pupa transforms into a butterfly. However, during the pupa stage, several factors can occur that will hinder metamorphosis from taking place, such as exposure to pesticides (like insect growth regulators), parasites, malnutrition, extreme temperature fluctuations, physical damage to the pupa, and environmental disruptions that interfere with the natural process of transformation. This is how I see ASD. An alteration occurring during pregnancy that only permits the transition of an organism from its larva to its pupa and then prevents further development into the butterfly - no or incomplete metamorphosis. The pupa stage is a world of its own; with enormous potentials and strengths. Yet, it becomes limited by its inability to fully function in the "butterfly" world. At that point, it may either die prematurely or develop abnormalities, making it very vulnerable. Autistic children experience a mutation at some

4

stage that causes a neurodivergence in their brains making it challenging to fully function like regular kids.

Attention Deficit Hyperactivity Disorder – ADHD

Psychiatrist Dr. ED Hallowell PhD of Harvard Medical school said "people with ADHD have a Ferrari for a brain but bicycle brakes. Strengthen the brakes and they have incredible power." I would like to think this applies to every other spectrum and special needs, not limited to ADHD. Wait until you realise Michael Jordan, Paris Hilton, Will Smith, Winston Churchill, Britney Spears etc all belong to this same WhatsApp group - attributing their success to their ADHD. People with ADHD develop an extreme curiosity about things and life in general.

ADHD is not a disease that needs to be cured. It's a unique brain wiring that can be harnessed for success. To make them fit into the world, shine and leverage their Ferrari brains; to find, explore and develop their own unique talents, we will have to target the natural root cause of the problem. What most people don't know is that our bodies have a natural calming system called the parasympathetic calming nervous system; responsible for slowing down our heart rates and reducing stress when we feel overwhelmed.

With the ADHD brain, there's an imbalance in the system which doesn't activate when it should. Hence, small

5

amounts of stress can lead to larger amounts of problems like hyperactivity, meltdowns and impulsive behaviours. Short term medications can be effective but they don't affect the root cause of the problem. Hence, when you start taking it, behaviour can get even worse than before. The most effective way to activate the body's natural calming system. Occupational therapists do this with a technique called deep pressure therapy; applying a constant pressure around the body which tells the brain it's safe and secure. This activates the entire nervous system and calms the body down.

Over time, parents have devised more local and effective ways of managing at home. Meaning, we can actually turn this ADHD into a super power. When a kid is out of control, most parents yell back, set consequences or even punish them. This will only trigger ADHD or make it worse. This is because, during this intense moment, their thinking brains are too overwhelmed to process whatever you are saying. That's why it feels like they don't understand consequences and won't take any rule seriously and if you punish them, it can lead to anxiety or even damage your relationship with your child.

With JB, I've found myself most times stuck in the vicious cycle of constantly yelling at him and many self-promises not to do it again. Imagine the guilt that sets in after yet another session of yelling. It reveals more of my intolerance and impatience than JB's ADHD excesses. However, I later found out, I would rather help him unlock his hyperfocal state and minimise his impulsive outburst, which I did. How? Let's talk about the traits first.

AUTISM (ASD) & ADHD EXPLAINED
(The Voltage Effect)

Understand, JB was equally diagnosed with ADHD about two years after his Autism diagnosis. Meaning, he currently has Autism & ADHD. Yes, it is possible to have both ADHD and ASD. Research shows that about 14% of children with ADHD also have autism, and 50-70% of people with autism also have ADHD. This would mean, double the challenges compared to those on just one of them. I'd however noticed it prior to the second diagnosis and just like I always say, "as a parent, trust your instincts with your kids". So, in this chapter, I'll talk predominantly about Autism but equally touch on ADHD and its traits.

Now, This is my understanding of what ASD and ADHD combine, look and feel like. We all (those in/from Africa, especially) must have experienced low/high voltage of electricity at least once. This occurs when the electrical current running through your electronics loses some of its energy due to too much pressure or gains energy due to less pressure. This can happen for a variety of reasons including long wire runs, undersized wiring, or too many electrical devices connected to a single circuit. Understand, most appliances and electronics are designed to operate within a specific voltage range. If/when the voltage drops/increases, these devices have to work harder/lesser to function properly. This can therefore reduce their efficiency and lifespan, data loss, overheating, motor damage etc. Meaning, if a household uses 100 volts of electricity to power all its electrical appliances, once there is a drop in voltage (low voltage) to say 20 volts, these same appliances are all forced to still operate with very minimal electricity. Most of the appliances will either not function or they will underperform. This is Autism explained. Once there is low voltage (limited energy), the brain will still function but it will underperform. Cognitive activities like thinking, memory and attention will decrease as the brain prioritises essential functions and may operate in low power mode where processing is slower and less efficient.

On the other hand, if a household requires 100 volts of electricity to power its appliances, and rather has 200 volts (for instance), there is an electrical potential enough to cause damages (high voltage). This is ADHD explained.

Once there is too high voltage (too much energy), the brain becomes overwhelmed leading to hyperactivity and lack of focus, tantrums and possible melt downs.

Once there is a disruption in this to-and-fro communication from the brain to the rest of the body, it causes a disorder - a direct opposite of what should normally happen. So, instead of telling you what they have seen, they will rather over perform or underperform. At that stage, the mouth is overpowered or underpowered for speech to happen, the nerves directly linked to the ears are overpowered or underpowered to bring out hearing sound. Same thing with the rest of the body. Since the body is not dead, there has got to be an interpretation of whatever is going on in their surroundings and again, the low/high voltage effect gets their system crowded with unexpressed/overexpressed emotions and actions leading to what is referred to as ASD and/or ADHD.

Autism (Special Needs) – The Ingenuity of God's Creation

Psalm 139:14 says, *"I praise you, for I am fearfully and wonderfully made: marvellous are thy works; and that my soul knoweth right well"* (New International Version). As

9

a Christian, a devout at that, I've often faced the dilemma of when to express my Faith in God's abilities and my Belief in His Divine purpose. God is too big to be fully understood; so, while Joseph in Genesis is trusting God for a release from Prison as a sign of God's power, God is busy extending the prison sentence to adequately prepare his throne room. How do we distinguish a prison sentence that is meant to destroy us and that which is meant to uplift us?

The number of Christian folks - who, in a bid to be kind, question my intensity with prayers, my profoundness with God's word and my consistency in following a popular early morning online ministry, are countless. Many will opt to join me in prayers while others will secretly do so. I do not by any means invalidate their faith and concerns. Of course, I've been there, done that and do appreciate the genuine efforts to see change and progress. I'm equally not sure of how best to communicate the fact that God's Divine Timing is ultimate and He remains God, Autism or not. I'm more interested in the purpose for which JB was born this way and what message, plans and purpose God has for him. "For I know that ALL THINGS work together for good, to them that love God and are called according to His purpose". In the above verse, David - the man after God's heart, expresses his understanding about God's diversity in creation; how God created humans in a way that is distinct and unique from other creations, and that no two people are exactly alike. Talk about God's ingenuity in creation.

I'd like to think, God in his divine wisdom, factored in varieties in creation. Life would be less fun if everyone was the same, don't you think? We can choose to be religious and see autism/special needs as a demonic attack or we can choose to be Spiritual and see it as another dimension of God's creations and mankind's purpose. Having lived with JB all his life and experienced first-hand his ingenuity, I strongly believe that autistic people have unique spiritual and supernatural qualities that allow them to perceive things that others cannot. It cannot be ordinary, much less an attack. I am a firm believer in purpose and I believe persons with Special Needs are here for purpose; to fulfil it and have others accomplish theirs.

According to Dr. Hugh Ross - Canadian Astrophysicist and Christian Apologist, "*Autism is a gift that God can and will use*". That autism is manifested as a spectrum should come as no surprise. God created every human being with unique characteristics, features, and behaviours that are manifested in no other human. Even identical twins are distinct from one another in many discernible ways. From a biblical perspective, we discern

11

that God created and designed every human being to fulfil a unique purpose that has eternal significance. Therefore, he made each one of us distinct from the rest of humanity. Of course, I still pray for him and daily speak the word of God upon him (Psalm 23 especially). Do I wish to hear him speak? Most definitely! Do I believe in miracles? Certainly! Nevertheless, I'm more interested in God's Will and Purpose for JB and regardless of the outcome, I will never love my son any less or think otherwise of God love for him.

Challenges of ASD/ADHD

To know them is to understand them and to understand them is to assist them. The challenges of ADS/ADHD get severe as they advance in ages especially when undiagnosed. Early diagnosis will mean early intervention to minimise these challenges. 60% of Kids with ADHD/ASD eventually get older without outgrowing - they grow into Autistic adults. Actually, the majority in Africa live and die without ever having a diagnosis, much less knowing they were on a spectrum. Sadly, the community further compounds the situation with gross ignorance on the subject leaving these persons worse off than they met. Someone with ASD/ADHD who doesn't get the proper diagnosis or support can have academic struggles and an increased prevalence of depression and anxiety. They may also have higher rates of imprisonment, divorce, driving accidents, unemployment, suicidal thoughts and behaviours, and other mental health issues. The good news is, some of us are intentional about sensitising the public; constantly teaching to wipe out the ignorance in our people thereby strengthening their bicycle brakes to harness their incredible power.

1. **Communication Difficulties:**

Whether verbal or non-verbal, communication is a huge challenge with ASD/ADHD kids, ranging from speaking to body language, using words appropriately, and having proper conversations. JB is non-verbal and even with speech and language therapy, he's not had too much improvement. At best, he'll exhibit echolalia with a clear indication he's unsure of what he's saying. Strange enough, he can sing and whilst at it, he pronounces every word, says the alphabet from A-Z and Z-A, counts from 1 to 100, and even spells some words including his name. It takes continuously repeating and doing a particular activity for him to get the cues and 7 out of 10 times, he will forget. Getting especially the non-verbal ones to master a couple of words can be quite challenging and will require enormous time.

2. Insecurities:

ASD/ADHD persons often second guess themselves. They are afraid of being judged and labelled, hence will rather not express their concerns. They have seen you laugh at others that look and sound like them; you'll laugh at them too. These stigmas and stereotypes can make them feel less about themselves, which can influence their self-esteem. They'll rather struggle with it their entire life than share their concerns with random people. It will take you much patience and tolerance to cope with them and once they develop trust in you (can feel sad and not judged), they open up and you'll be amazed by how much they'll reveal about themselves (again, verbal or non-verbal).

3. Very Few or No Friends:

ASD/ADHD usually live in isolation and will make one or few friends in a lifetime. They expect negative experiences to repeat in every friendship and face difficulties moving on from past experiences, and disclosing their autism to others. They have trust issues and would rather believe themselves than the most convincing facts out there. JB literally sees me as his only friend. He struggles with severe communication and social difficulties and that makes it difficult for him to make and keep friends. I'm literally his best friend and he seemingly doesn't need another. He depends on me for every aspect of Friendship and still wants his Mother when the need arises. Now, that can be overwhelming but the love is real.

4. **Expressing Emotions:**

They come across as selfish and cold with their belongings and emotions. They rarely express emotions the conventional way and might seem insensitive to the emotions of others.

During my depression days with JB (read more about this in the chapters ahead), I'll cry most days, I'll shed tears and sob. He'll look at me and be indifferent. No iota of concern nor response to my emotions. Sometimes, I felt neglected. Yes, as a mother, doing everything by myself, I needed emotional support and because my then husband was not around and available, JB was the only one I truly relied on emotionally. I wanted to know he sees my tears and understands what I'm going through. I needed him to at least cry or show some emotions towards whatever it is I was dealing with. He didn't. I assumed he had zero empathy, didn't care and was only concerned about himself.

Knowing all I know now, I was wrong. Autistic persons can truly experience pain and even share the emotions of others. The difference is in their expression of it. They might look away just like when they avoid eye contact but they truly feel the pain and hurt from within. They equally show concern, affection and love too. Again, they just have a different way of doing it.

5. **Sensory Challenges:**

They are very sensitive to bright lights, loud noises, crowded places and weird sounds. Some are hyper sensitive while others are hypo sensitive and can affect their sight, taste, smell, touch, balance and body awareness. Their response to this is usually putting a finger in both ears or screaming, perceiving the smell of their food before they will eat, rejecting food just at first taste or glance, shaky handwriting, sometimes numb to pain, and walking in an unstable or a zigzag manner as their motor skills are usually affected (fine and gross).

JB loves me! Actually, he's obsessed about his mum. I know he does, not because he says so, his actions prove it. He will share his space and toys with me, very willing to play with me, will cry hysterically each time I have to leave him behind and "fights" when he sees another child in his territory (if I dare carry another). His smiles, hugs and laughter are usually seen only when he truly cares about someone. I'm blessed to experience such unadulterated love from him, though non-verbal.

"Let's focus on what people with autism can do, rather than what they can't"
[National Autistic Society]

DIARY OF A SPECIAL MUM

CHAPTER 2:

BREAKING THE STEREOTYPES

"Autism is not a tragedy, ignorance is!"

[Author Unknown]

Stereotypes towards Special Needs are common.

Recognizing autism as a natural part of human diversity is the first step to breaking stereotypes. This is only possibly by celebrating the unique strengths and abilities of these individuals and these strengths are enormous. Challenging negative stereotypes and stigma associated with autism is the only way we get to fully embrace them, understand and celebrate them for their uniqueness while sensitising and creating more awareness. The ignorance is real! Education is needed. My approach towards the stigma and discrimination is to educate everyone and anyone who cares to listen. I cannot possibly match the negative energy. I was once ignorant too; I always remind myself of that. In retrospect, I see the many special needs we grew up with and most times, I wish to turn back the hands of time to relate with them better. Breaking these stereotypes about autism, will entail challenging and debunking the misconceptions that exist. This is possible via showcasing the complexity and uniqueness of the autism spectrum; highlighting the individuality and unique strengths of individuals on the spectrum.

Prior to this book release, I'd become intentional at doing live shows on TikTok and Facebook; sharing my story and journey while promoting accurate and diverse representations of autism in media and cultural discourse. The stigma is real, I've had my fair share of it. However, education will help us all, move away from such stigmas and instead embrace narratives that reflect the multifaceted nature of autism. This is a clarion call to my fellow Africans (especially), to join me in this sensitisation by creating more awareness campaigns and fostering a more inclusive society that values and supports the contributions and potentials of all individuals, regardless of their neurodiversity; enabling them to thrive and become the best versions of themselves. Let's begin by looking at all what ASD is not and later look at what it is from the plethora of theories and experiences.

1. **Autism is NOT a Disease/Illness:**

Let me borrow the words of Dr. Hugh Ross - Canadian astrophysicist, Christian apologist, and old-Earth creationist, "ASD should not be labelled as a disorder, a handicap, or a genetic defect. A better word would be neurotypical (or neurodivergent). For autistic people, some neurological functions are more challenging than for neurotypical people, while several others may be easier. This distinction is evident as well for other neurodivergent people, such as those with attention deficit hyperactivity disorder (ADHD)." Ever heard of the phrase "disability (a term I deliberately avoid using, though medically approved) is just another ability? Sounds cliché but true. Autism is a lifelong condition that results from the brain developing differently than in non-autistic people. It's not a disease, but rather a different way of processing information and environmental stimuli. Many autistic adults feel that autism is part of who they are, and that there are many positive aspects to value. If you consider them sick, you will undermine their strength and pamper their excesses. You won't be able to draw a line between the spectrum and stubbornness. You will downplay discipline which is highly needed. Of course, you can't discipline a sick person, can you? It is not a disease but a disorder. Meaning, the brain is not sick but just functions differently.

A disease is a medical condition with a specific cause, recognizable symptoms, and a defined process. Diseases can affect the whole body or part of it, and can be caused by viruses, bacteria, fungi, protozoa, or worms. While a disorder is a group of symptoms that disrupt normal physical or mental functions, but without a known cause. Disorders can be characterized by functional impairment, but they don't necessarily involve structural change. I don't ever look at JB and think he's sick. Rather, I'm marvelled each day by the constant display of his ingenuity; a genius at work.

2. **Autistic Children are NOT Witches/Wizards:**
   Growing up in Africa, it was common to see many of these kids labelled "Evil". In Cameroon, the term "Ogbanje" would mean an evil child who has come with the sole objective to destroy a family; Financially, Spiritually, Mentally and otherwise. Some Africans till this day believe Autistic (Special Needs) kids are not ordinary and so, cannot co-exist with others; therefore, experience open discrimination and lack of empathy. Some are constantly subjected to traditional rights, inhumane treatment and torture, such as dropping them by river

banks at night and instructed to return to where they are coming from. Imagine a toddler in the dark by a river having to spend at least one night alone. Imagine the pains the parents of these kids are/were subjected to; having to watch your child(ren) go through such, yet unable to rescue them from such barbarism.

3. **They are NOT a punishment for your past sins or present character by God:**

Though a self-conscious emotion, emanating from our value systems, Guilt terribly aggravates pain and quite often prevents us from seeing the light at the end of the tunnel. To think God will "punish" an innocent kid just to get at you, for whatever wrong you did in the past is clearly a show of ignorance on God's personality. Jesus heals a man who had been blind from birth and when questioned if his infirmity was as a result of sin, Jesus responded, *"Neither this man nor his parents sinned, but it was so that the works of God might be displayed and illustrated in him."* (John 9:1-5 (Amplified Bible). The works of God herein would mean Purpose, hence staying guilty for whatever wrong you committed in the past would be a disservice to oneself and a complete waste of time.

Away from being religious, let's be more logical. A good number of Autists/Special Needs are geniuses - inventing the most wonders in the universe. In such circumstances, are we then saying, God punished or blessed the parents of these geniuses? Voilà! If anything, these are Special Kids with Special Needs given to Special Parents for a Special Purpose. I don't know about you, but this is absolutely how I feel about JB and I.

4. **Autism is Not from Vaccines:**

I can literally feel someone fighting me whilst reading this. I recall during my early sensitisation days on social media, a couple of Parents were in denial of this point. I used to be too. I could swear JB's Autism started only when he had the MMR vaccine and just like many other parents with such a mindset, I deprived him of any other form of vaccines for fear of the unknown. I was wrong! I was in grief and had to put the blame on someone or something to feel better. I do not invalidate anyone's experiences as vaccines have been known to cause harm in kids especially when not properly administered. However, Research Scientists have in no way associated any discoveries of Autism directly linked to Autism.

According to the 2024 Immunisation Safety Reviews, since 2003, there have been nine CDC-funded or conducted studies that have found no link between thimerosal-containing vaccines and ASD. These studies also found no link between the measles, mumps, and rubella (MMR) vaccine and ASD in children. In fact, no links have been found between any vaccine ingredients and ASD.

5. **Mildness does NOT Mean less severity:**

Mild Autism, otherwise referred to as Asperger's syndrome, is the spectrum of less pronounced Autism symptoms making it easier to mask or overlook. In the words of Adam Walton "Mild autism doesn't mean one experiences autism mildly. It means YOU experience their autism mildly. You may not know how hard they've had to work to get to the level they are."

"Delly, your son doesn't look autistic" is what I get each time I get to post JB's pictures/videos on social media. I know this is meant to be a compliment but again, it will be a disservice to everyone on the spectrum; especially those with more physically mild autism, yet enormous internal challenges. So, no! I'd rather you don't say that. Just like JB, many Special Kids are treated unfairly or overly pampered because of assumptions about their looks. Autism is more of what goes on in the brain, spinal cord and nervous system. It is less physical. Looks can be deceptive and should not be relied upon to treat Autist. Yes, JB is a charmer; has been since birth. Matter of fact, the camera really doesn't do him much justice. However, he has enormous challenges ranging from speech impairment, motor skills difficulties, ADHD, limited social interaction than some ASD kids with more physical challenges. Don't limit him to his looks otherwise you'll miss the opportunity to be educated and to accord him the required help he needs.

6. **Autistic people have a special talent:**
   understand, autism is not just about challenges. There are also extraordinary potentials. However, while many renowned geniuses and talented people have been said to be on the spectrum, it is not true for all cases. While these examples are usually used to console and encourage parents with special kids, it could on the other hand be misleading; giving them

false hope. While we teach Parents help bring out the very best in their kids, this "best" must not necessarily be in talent form. It could just be as simple as understanding potty training, managing emotions better or even as basic as responding to their names.

As a special parent, my approach towards my son JB is first and foremost love, acceptance, tolerance and encouragement. Any talent he exhibits is only a plus. I'm interested in recklessly loving him and giving him the best support possible. To just wake up every day and see his cute smile, follow up on his routine and kiss him good night, surpasses any talent he could possibly have. Being autistic doesn't necessarily make one the next Albert Einstein. As a result, it is unadvisable to put your child in competition with other kids. We all have strengths and weaknesses and autistic people are no different. If you can't find talent in them, find love.

7. **Autism can be cured:**

This is very tricky as most people's hopes will be shattered. It will be unfair of me to raise your hopes; however small. So, categorically and medically speaking, autism cannot be cured (at least, not yet). Science is still trying to place a finger on exactly how best to eradicate it. Until then, it remains one of the modern mysteries. Oh well, I know what you're thinking now. "What God cannot do, does not exist." Absolutely! I am a Christian and a firm believer in God being miraculous and merciful. I believe God is bigger than autism and if He wills, with faith, we will record a miracle - cure for autism. What I often tell my fellow Christian folks is, pray, have faith in the word of God, speak the word over your child(ren), be a loving parent to your kid, support their endeavours and leave the rest to God. If the desired miracle comes, fine! If not, I will never love my son any less. Again, autism is only managed via early intervention, medications, lifestyle modifications. Research shows 40% of children diagnosed with autism, outgrow autism at some stage while the rest 60 eventually grow into autistic adults. Until there's been an official communique, maybe from your doctor and reputable outlets, about a cure for autism, I'll advise give autistic people the support and services they need to live a happy, healthy and long life and not pressure them to be what we want them to be.

CHAPTER 3:

PRE AND POST TRAITS OF AUTISM

"Autism is not a tragedy, ignorance is!"
[Author Unknown]

Understandably, not every child reaches a language or mobile milestone at the same rate, even though their respective speaking develops simultaneously with other aspects of growth like walking. So many babies say their first words around the time they start walking. If after 26 to 30 months your kid isn't speaking yet; trying to form sentences of at least 2 or 3 words, you'll be right to be concerned. Though delayed speech or overall development is not necessarily a sign of ASD, it is advisable to go in for a Speech evaluation, Developmental screening or Hearing tests once you start noticing such tendencies.

Regressive tendencies (stopped doing the things he already could do). At just one year, kids are already quite active. With JB, it was quite easy to spot such changes as he was quite bubbly and then suddenly became the opposite. I could easily tell something was wrong. JB was diagnosed with ASD and Regressive tendencies. Meaning, he learns

29

new things (much slower than other kids his age) and later forgets them. He gets to a new level and after a while, he falls back and below. He could start counting from one to a hundred and later go back to counting from one to ten. He starts up a positive habit and before long, he stops it and could jump on the direct opposite. As earlier mentioned, before the age of two, he was already muttering words when suddenly he stopped and was mute for so long before some words came back.

1. **Speech Impairment and Hyper Fixation:**

Silence and long stare on objects characterised this phase. At two, JB went mute. He wouldn't say anything and not act as though he wanted to. He lost his smile and would take a long stare at the wall or an object. He became very unresponsive to his name and other gestures. He looked sad and gloomy. I noticed and assumed it was either tiredness or a change of environment. I'd just picked up a part time job which entailed dropping him off a Minder for hours. I assumed he was uncomfortable with his new environment. The lady equally noticed and asked if I'd noticed any of such changes. She will call the once lively JB over and over and not a response from him. He won't even look towards whoever was calling. Sometimes, he only looked once he heard me calling; my voice. Even at that, no smile, no excitement. He was quite gloomy. I was worried but kept assuming it was a phase.

2. **Hyperactivity:**

Jumping nonstop for hours (2y.0). They never sit still and are constantly bagging off the wall. Their energy levels are usually above the top. JB, regained excitement at some point but in an usual way. He had started playing again but this time, by himself. He would jump for hours non-stop. He didn't seem tired at any point. Even when I tried stopping him, he'll resist and keep at it. Initially, I assumed it was the excitement of a bouncy bed. However, he even jumped on the couch and kept jumping. This time around, I could tell something was not right.

3. **Loss of Eye Contact:**

JB would usually give you eye contact accompanied with his broad smile. He equally lost it. He'd show his face while turning his eyes elsewhere. He was deliberate at not looking in my eyes. He'd gained some jumping skulls but lost eye contact. It was quite challenging and disturbing dealing with this new development, so I tried forcing him by turning his head towards my direction and he would cry or scream. So, I stopped. Upon research, I realised eye contact requires a lot of brain power for them; making it hard to process information in their brains thereby making them anxious.

Social communication is obviously a big deal and avoiding eye contact is their way of saying no to sensory overload. Without eye contact, there's hardly Speech development and social skills; facial expressions and body language. Every child is different and so, your child might require a unique approach to getting help. With JB, he was more comfortable looking or facing elsewhere while listening to me. Sometimes playing with an object while I'm talking. I noticed he was less anxious with that especially as he was non-verbal.

During therapy, we were given some tips on how to manage or improve the situation in the most compassionate and ethical way. Some of which included:

- Pausing in the middle of an activity or conversation to initiate eye contact. It builds curiosity and he's forced to know why the pause thereby giving eye contact.

- Engaging in their favourite subject or activities. It builds trust and re-enforces eye contact.
- Encourage them when they accomplish a task of eye contact. It is quite reinforcing. It could mean giving them a "Hi5", a gift or just a verbal "well done".
- Practice making eye contact with others: Children learn more from what they see us do than what we tell them. Do more eye contact with others. They are watching even when it doesn't look like it.
- Visual support: This worked best with JB. Making gestures around my eyes that propelled him to replicate. Repeatedly pointing my finger close to his eyes while taking them back to mine. It became more of an activity he wanted to engage in.

4. **Temper Tantrums & Meltdowns:**

This usually happens when they don't get their way. They can go from sweet and caring to angry, yelling and banging in a matter of minutes. It is their way of expressing frustration and disappointment. This is usually caused by communication difficulties, sensory overload and attention seeking and unlike other kids, theirs can last 10 minutes to an hour. The longer it takes, the more aggressive he gets. Understanding the triggers help a great deal. It can be quite risky and driving with an autistic child throwing tantrums. I've almost had accidents many times, but for the Mercy and Grace of God. You get confused between trying to calm him down vs focusing on the steering while he keeps screaming. You don't want to stay around JB when he has tantrums. He would scream, hit the wall, floor or anyone by him. He gets really uncontrollable and would scatter things around. I can't count the number of TV remotes I've had to replace. Sometimes, it is replacing the TV because he smashed it during a meltdown. It could be just anything he has access to when angry. However, I learnt later that:

- Maintaining my calmness even as he melts down is quite necessary. I used to freak out but not anymore.
- Taking breaks from whatever activity so he doesn't feel overburdened.

- I try not to change his routine except when necessary. Autistic children are used to routines and it can get them struggling once anything gets altered.

- Knowing when to exit an environment he's not very comfortable with or setting the environment conducive enough for him to be OK with. JB loves Church! He can't wait to play the drums after the sermon. He likes to run around and get hugs from his favourite Uncles and only comes around me when it's time to leave. The least delay gets him upset and until we leave he will be calm.

- Identifying his needs and making provision for them, when and how he prefers them. With JB, a pack of potato or plantain crisps does the trick most often.

5. **Lack of Focus:**

Few years after JB was diagnosed with ASD, he was equally diagnosed with ADHD (Attention Deficit Hyperactivity Disorder) mainly characterised by the lack of focus, no impulse control and very limited concentration on whatever activity. These are common traits in kids but it is a lot more frequent and extreme with autistic kids than most kids their age. JB struggles to focus on any task for more than 15 seconds. He does what he wants, when he wants and how he wants. He equally struggles with himself while doing so. Actually, he starts throwing a tantrum if you insist otherwise. However, he'll stay for hours on a toy or phone, snapping pictures and taking videos of his flickering fingers. You dare not stop him.

LATER TRAITS

1. **Lining up Things in Very Orderly Manner (3 years)**

   He'd lost the constant jumping, improved on eye contact but suddenly gained some kind of organisation of objects. This would include shoes, toys or just anything he fancies. He'll line up his things in a very orderly manner and would stare at them in accomplishment.

2. **Using Fingers to Close his Ears to Avoid Listening to you (4 years):**

   This is a coping mechanism for most autistic persons. Their own way of expressing disapproval to someone or something or stop an irritating sound or voice. I know he's uncomfortable when I see his hands in his ears. I know he detests someone when his first reaction is blocking his ears. JB blocks his ears before doing a wrong thing because he already knows he'll be stopped. The mere sight of my kid sister (Dilys) gets his hands on his ears. JB detests Dilys in a hilarious way. He's not happy she doesn't let him have his way. She's stricter with him and disciplines him a lil more than I do. She's JB's worst nightmare. Lol He places his hands in his ears just to let Dilys know "he's uninterested in whatever it is she has to say".

3. **Echolalia (Pathological):**

The immediate and involuntary repetition of words or sentences by kids made by others. Echolalia is quite common with kids over the ages of 2 - 3 normal with language development, helping them internalise and remember new words and phrases. Above 3, it is usually an indication of an **underlying problem; ASD or ADHD. It becomes pathological echolalia if it persists.** Just like they like doing things routinely, echolalia is more of a routine way of speaking. It is usually caused by their need and desire for sensory overload, self-talk and prefabrication. Ask JB a question and instead of him responding, he repeats the same words; of course, with/without understanding the meaning. It could be immediate, delayed, interactive and non-interactive and interestingly, I've witnessed JB with all forms.

Example of immediate Echolalia:

Mum: JB, will you eat?

JB: "JB will you eat?"

Me: Bring my phone.

JB: "Phone, phone" or "Bringa Pho". He repeats whatever is said even though he can't properly pronounce some of the words. *Delayed echolalia* is when he goes silent when spoken to and after minutes or hours, he repeats those words

to himself. Example:

Mum: Good morning JB

JB: (Mute and facing elsewhere)

JB (1 hour later): "Good morning, good morning, good morning, good morning."

JB expresses echolalia especially when he detests a particular activity which is being imposed on him. He's overly sensitive to the sound of a shaving machine on his head, the feel of a towel or hard sponge on his body. Hence, I would regurgitate and recite everything that comes to mind at that point. A typical display of Echolalia by JB when having a haircut or bath. The moment he sets eyes on a shaving machine, he immediately starts screaming and trying to escape, and when he can't have his way, he starts reciting everything saved in his memory. "One to forty and then skips to ninety-nine, one hundred. The wheels on the bus go round round round, round round round, round round round. The wheels on the bus go round round round, all through the town. Baabaa Black sheep, have you any wool, yes Sir, yes Sir, three bags full, one for the master and one for the dame, one for the little boy who lives down the lane. A, B, C, D, E, F, G, H, I, J, K, L, M, N, O, P, Q, R, S, T, U, V, W, X, Y, Z. Imela, Imela, okaka, Onyiekeruwa, Imela, Imela Eze-mo. One, two, three, four, five, six, seben (for seven), eight, nine, tennnnnn (for 10). 41, 42, 43, 44, 45, 46, 47, 48, 99, 100.

Hi, I am Peppa Pig, this is my little brother George, this is mummy Pig and this is daddy Pig. Peppa Pig (accompanied by the pig's sound (oink oink). Z, Y, X, W, V, U, T, S, R, Q, P, O, N, M, L, K, J, I, H, G, F, E, D, C, B, A.

He doesn't stop until you do and he does so at the top of his voice. As stressful as carrying out his personal care could be in such a circumstance, it is usually a moment for me to have a really good laugh. JB is a handful and sweetheart, indeed. Echolalia is a step towards developing language and communication skills. It is their own way of saying YES to what is asked, interacting with others, drawing attention or showing dissatisfaction. Thereafter, they gradually outgrow echolalia and start using their own words and phrases

4. **Chewing Portions of his Clothes or Objects (5 years old):**

Again, this is a coping mechanism for autistic persons with sensory overload which aids them to focus and pay attention. It is their own way of managing stress due to the deficiencies they have processing information and coping with anxiety. It's frustrating each time that happens as it literally damages the object or the outfit. Each time JB has done that, I've had to discard the outfit. That's how severe it is. It is actually not premeditated; they just do it unconsciously because of sensory needs. Sometimes, I've only had to keep him engaged and busy as this can equally be caused by boredom or provide a safe alternative like chew toys or snacks and get him distracted.

5. **Poor Motor Skills:**

Motor skill development has to do with forming complex connections between different parts of the brain that link sensory information from the body with information from the environment, plus our innate motivation in order to plan and execute motor movements. In simple terms, it means the ability of the body to move and perform tasks like walking, running, writing. For this to happen, the body's nervous system, muscles and brain have to all work together.

Kids with autism often struggle with poor motor skills which can range from mild to severe; holding a pen properly to write or draw, holding cutlery well enough to eat. JB till this day is still spoon-fed. He does well eating handy food but struggles with using cutlery, so he's always assisted. There's been such great improvements and it gets better daily. He could barely write but was quite passionate about writing and drawing anywhere and everywhere. He'd watched so many cartoons and learnt a great deal from it and I didn't know he could do so well. The most I'd seen him do was scribble uncoordinated and "meaningless" lines on a paper. It was my birthday and I'd just gifted myself a designer handbag (D&G). Lo and behold, JB took a pen and wrote "stuvwxyz", in such beautiful handwriting. I heard him reciting but I couldn't imagine he was equally writing. I'd never seen him write so, I assumed he couldn't. I was gripped with such mixed feelings; happy he was finally getting his grip and angry my designer bag was ruined. To my surprise, he had beautiful handwriting and was quite orderly.

6. **Difficult Social Interaction:**

Always in their corner, further from other kids. They decide their games, play by themselves and refuse sharing a space with the rest. They will not share their toys with anyone and will hardly make eye contact when spoken to. They detest being interrupted and could go for long periods by themselves. Their only friends are usually their mums or guardians. Language and communication is usually a big deal for them, I guess they prefer not to stress others or be stressed. I'm JB's bestie. He always wants to be with me.. Since he's quite clingy, I've come up with games which involve taking turns, following rules, imitation and eye contact. I equally reinforce the little things he does. It builds confidence in him and gets him coming for more. A hi-5 boosts his ego up and he'll sometimes initiate it after accomplishing a task.

7. **Fussy Eating:**

JB was initially a foodie. He's now a foodie. This wasn't always the case. When he turned two, he lost appetite for almost everything. This was the most stressful season of all. It's hard to deal with the situation as it is, harder to cope when a special child who can barely express himself, refuses food. He stopped drinking juice and till date only takes water. He'll perceive the smell of whatever I prepare for him to eat and immediately reject it. If he takes interest in any food, he'll eat only that for months. He became malnourished, lacked some vitamins, yet would not take multivitamins either. Quite a nightmare for every mother. I watched him grow lean by the day but couldn't help.

For more than three years, JB lived on yoghurt & potato crisps for snacks and cereal (fruit and fibre) for breakfast, lunch and dinner. He drinks only water till date. JB later started eating okro (draw) soup and any starch. I made okro and garri for more than a year. He had free school lunch vouchers but wouldn't join the others to eat.

When my kid sister came over to join us, his eating improved greatly. She cooked all kinds of spicy African foods and imposed them on him. It was such a hassle at the beginning. JB would pin his teeth together and wouldn't let anything get to his mouth. My sister insisted and he started opening his mouth for the food he would chew or swallow. He'll hold the food in his mouth and spit it out immediately he gets the chance. It was the consistency of my sister for me. She didn't give up. JB eventually got tired of fighting and started eating. Initially, just a few spoons and after a few months, he became such a foodie. Now, there's hardly anything he doesn't eat. However, JB rather took her for his number one enemy. He gained his appetite and found a new enemy. See chapter 6 for more.

8. **Tip toeing:**

Studies show that 9% of ASD children walk on their toes. As much as the exact cause of this is unknown, fingers greatly point towards one of the most irritating traits of Autists. I can't count the number of times I've had to stretch JB's feet and toes just so he can stand and walk properly. He'll tiptoe sometimes all week. When you think he's over it, he starts again. The many shoes and socks I've had to buy; they get destroyed really fast. See, autism is quite interesting in a stressful way. Lol. I was more concerned when he suddenly started developing tendons (built muscles) at the back of his legs. I got so uncomfortable and tried everything to stop it. Sadly, JB didn't stop and I'm getting used to it, while hoping he outgrows it.

9. **Sleep Disorders:**

Quite common with Special Kids due to anxiety, sensory overload or food allergies making it hard for them to fall asleep or stay asleep. With JB, I didn't stress on this and quite frankly, I give God praise for this particular aspect. JB sleeps like the baby he is. Sleeps all through the night and even snores. Strange enough, realised he has a 7 hours sleep routine and will auto wake up once it is 7 hours. If he starts sleeping at 7pm, he automatically wakes up at 2am, if he goes to sleep at 12 midnight, he wakes up at exactly 7am. Meaning, if for any reason he sleeps early, I'm certain to be awake most part of the night. Hence, I'll insist he stays awake most times till 11pm so he wakes up at 6am and get ready for school. Without which, he'll either wake up late or too early.

Now imagine having to deal with another Parent whose kid(s) has such a sleep disorder. Such Parents might constantly sleep-walk/talk at odd times. It is as difficult as it gets. I recall being frustrated most nights when I'd not mastered his sleeping pattern. Once he's up, he immediately starts jumping or banging. There's no way you can find time to sleep or be fully awake during the day. I'll advise you to get enough physical exercise, eat well and avoid caffeine and too much screen before bedtime. If it persists, see your doctor on prescription for medications to treat insomnia in autistic kids.

10. **Potty Training:**

My worst nightmare! Lordy Lord! Where do I start from? Of all the traits; temporal and permanent, Potty training, I'd say, has been the most challenging for me. Learning to use the toilet, particularly in a way that others see as appropriate, can be a challenge for some autistic children. It is imperative to note that dealing with the difficulties of autistic children should be handled from both the spectrum and the medical angle. Meaning, a child might be suffering from constipation for instance but unable to communicate it, given he/she is autistic. Otherwise, we will frustrate them further into a mess, especially during potty training. According to Lorraine MacAlister - an autism training consultant for The National Autistic Society and co-author of the book Toilet Training and the Autism Spectrum, *"There are a variety of different reasons why some autistic children can experience toileting difficulties. Some of these reasons might be linked to their autistic identity, their neurodivergence, specific health issues or physical difficulties. It can sometimes be a combination of factors, knowing when they need to use the toilet, communicating the need to use the toilet, learning to use different toilets, sensory and environmental challenges, wiping themselves, smearing their poop"*.

Guess what, JB struggled with all these and though there's been quite a significant improvement, it is still my greatest challenge with him. I watched YouTube videos (Poo goes to poo land), researched a lot, made enquiries, asked for assistance and still, it was quite challenging. I insisted on getting him to use the toilet pot. He got used to it and started doing number one and two. Though he was still struggling with wiping after "number two", you can only imagine the joy I felt at that stage. Massive improvement! I stopped using nappies and it was such a relief. Sometimes, he forgets and does it on him. Other times, he follows instructions and free times, he reminds himself to do the right thing. One thing I noticed was, when a Special Kid is overly focused on a hobby; gadgets and phones (especially) they tend to miss out on their routines. Each time JB is too immersed, watching cartoons or a favourite program, he does number one and two on him. Once their minds are engaged on what gets their attention, they tend to alter their routines. There are obviously more traits than I could write; each varying from one spectrum level to another. Whatever the case, see to it that you maintain a ROUTINE lifestyle for them, be patient and observant while hoping for the best.

CHAPTER 4:

STAGES OF GRIEF

"The chronic grief you feel as a parent of a special needs child is not debilitating. It's usually a quiet whisper in the back of your mind."

[Kate Divine McAnaney]

Grief? Oh yes! I still remember in one of our (I use "our" because I took the lessons quite seriously too) therapy sessions, I was asked how it feels like having an autistic child. As much as my response would be different now, I only gave the best response I felt appropriate at that time. That was truly how I felt. I responded with "I feel I have lost a child". I could feel the hurt in her facial expression. She literally held back her tears but I didn't hold mine; I couldn't hold them back. She let me cry out my heart and after a few minutes of sobbing, she gave me such a reassuring hug and assured me, I'll be fine. I had plans for my baby. How I wanted him to be, how he will dress, eat, stand, the kind of school he'll attend, how he'll pose for the camera, I had collections of all the beautiful pictures of gorgeous looking babies I found on the Internet. I could see a model in my mind; yes, a model for Jesus Christ and I intended to bring it out the best way possible. So yes, there's grief. Just like losing someone, this grief is not short lived - make no mistakes. It is quite real and the healing process is different for everyone.

After the hug, I was advised to let go of the child I'd expected and embrace the one I have. There's no way you can ever heal or truly love this child as he is deserving, if you do not bury the illusion in your head and welcome the reality in your heart. Those were the most bitter pills I've ever had to swallow in this journey. Of course, I cried; the pain was real, excruciating. I went home, reflected on all that was said and the possibility of it being my new normal. The pain intensified and depression got in. That time I knew it was time for a choice to be sane and embrace my new reality or depressed and lose him to the Social Services. Of course, I choose to be an awesome mum to my baby but not until these stages are completed.

Psychiatrist Elisabeth Kubler-Ross identified five stages of grief as far as dealing with pain or grief is concerned. Whether losing a loved one, breaking up from a relationship, being laid off from a job or dealing with a medical diagnosis as was the case with me, pain is pain and we all deal with it differently. We have different pain thresholds and there are no rules or time limit. You may return to an earlier stage of grief, such as depression or anger, throughout your life. Don't be shy about your pain. Express it the most you can. We all are exposed to different resources for healing and it will be silly and unfair to invalidate that of others for whatever reason. So, cry it out, lament, pour out the frustration, give yourself time. It is all part of therapy.

1. **Denial: Nothing is wrong with my son!**

Like I mentioned, I had plans for my son. When he was clinically diagnosed autistic, I immediately rejected the diagnosis. As a Christian, I quoted every scripture I could pertaining to good health. "I don't care what the doctor's reports are. I believe in the report of God for my son." "My son is OK", I kept telling myself. I tried to carry on like nothing happened and just keep on with my baby. Every attempt to get me to therapy by the Doctors was declined. I felt a kind of pain that only denial could compensate for. I had to stay in this stage for a while because accepting it would mean dealing with my worst nightmares. I used to teach Sunday School (kids) lessons in my local Church and some of these kids were autistic, so I understood how difficult communication was. Sometimes just having to deal with their tantrums and excesses was a big deal. "Does it mean my son will forever be the same and I'll have to live with such for the rest of my life? No way! My son is fine. He probably just has his own pace of growth and I need to exercise some patience with him."

It was time to enroll him in school. "My son cannot attend a special needs school. Nothing is wrong with him". I insisted and enrolled him in a mainstream school. I had my worst nightmares. He will cry all day once I drop him off until I pick him up. I kept telling myself, he'll pick up once he starts associating with other kids. I was wrong. He wasn't coping with the set up and the teachers weren't trained to handle special needs kids either. I kept insisting. The denial was real! I was angry, yet I was wrong!

Understandably, many of you are still at this stage and it is OK. Take your time and figure things out. Also, understand, the longer you stay in denial, the more difficult it is for your kid(s) to find themselves. It becomes challenging for them to exist in the set up you insist for them and because that setup does not align with their "world" they tend to

52

fight it. For instance, accepting my child is on the spectrum with ADHD would mean me taking appropriate measures; putting in place the structure and facilities to enable them thrive in their journey. Putting safety locks on the door, informing strangers of his condition so they treat him better, enrolling him in a special school that accommodates his needs etc. The reverse kept him frustrated and he devised means of coping which made management very challenging.

2. **Anger: The Blame Game!**

I was in denial and found myself crying most times. I had started to internalise what the Doctors and others were saying. I was angry at God. I didn't outrightly say it but deep within, I believed God failed me. This is not what he promised me. I'd received a prophetic word prior to being pregnant, that I will have a son who will be great amongst the nations. He will be a Financial Sponsor of the Gospel and his name will be highly solicited. After his birth, I received another word from a total stranger "he will play international soccer for England and will be a name highly sought after. As his mother, I will lay hands on my tummy and prophesy on him. I prayed throughout the pregnancy and declared greatness on him. His dad did the same and we couldn't for once envision anything short of a mighty man of valour. Where did I go wrong? What did I do to deserve this punishment? "Lord, I've been committed to serving you, I have treated other kids like they were mine, I've not done anything to a kid, looking back that warrants such payment on my child. I love children and have served as a nanny. I took care of Junior like he was mine. My primary purpose is in the ministry of orphans and vulnerable children. I gave to them even when I had very little or "nothing". With the little resources I had, I sacrificed to see them smile. Where did I go wrong to deserve such a burden from you, Lord?" I was angry, yet I was wrong!

I was angry and frustrated with others. I hated anyone who suggested anything relating to autism. I was quick to discard any suggestions by other special mums and it made me bitter. I'll ignore prayer links when sent to some WhatsApp groups I belong to, even when told about the many testimonies of Autistic kids being made whole. It just didn't sit well with me; perhaps, I was living in denial and anger, yet, I was wrong.

I was angry at my son; "he could have fought for us". I thought he was bent on punishing me for whatever reason. You could have said "no to autism" when it showed up but you didn't. I was angry at him. I remember one time strolling with him in his buggy, while he kept crying (JB was a cry baby; always crying as long as he was awake). I was tired, restless and helpless and in my frustration, I started lashing out on him. "If you didn't want me as your mother, you shouldn't have come to/through me. I don't know what I did to deserve this stress. I didn't kill my mother; you won't kill me". The frustration was real! A lady was passing nearby and overheard the bitterness oozing from my mouth. She couldn't hold herself and immediately rebuked me "he was in heaven and you invited him on earth. Stop blaming him for your choices". She added! I responded (still in pain), "He could have gone to other parents if he didn't like me this much". This lady could clearly read my frustrations and as a mother of older kids (I guess), she sure knew better to encourage me than engage in a "tug of words". Then calmly, she said "my daughter, I understand. This is a phase and it will soon pass, OK?". I nodded in agreement as tears rolled my eyes. It felt much better but still angry, yet I was wrong.

I was angry with myself! I constantly judged myself. I blamed myself for not being such a great mum. I'll compare myself to the seemingly awesome mums around. I amplified my errors and at some point, was sure, I would have done better to prevent the situation. I felt inadequate and thought "perhaps, it was all an error having a baby at this time". I doubted if the choice of returning to London without my husband was well thought of. I got married before having this baby not solely because the idea of being a single mum didn't align with my values but more so, the stress of raising a kid(s) alone - a job meant for at least two persons. It looked like my worst fears were coming to pass and I didn't know what to do. I was angry, yet, I was wrong!

I was angry with the NHS (National Health Service). I blamed them for being responsible. I was certain it was the BCG (Bacillus Calmette-Guérin) vaccine that brought this on my baby. I kept telling anyone who cared to listen not to vaccinate their kids anymore. I actually refused to go for the last vaccine when it was time. I was so angry but I was wrong!

I was angry at life; it was unfair. Why do bad things happen to good people? Oops! I'm nowhere near good. I was so angry, yet I was wrong!

The Doctor's reports started looking like my reality. Every research I did on Autism became noticeable. Sadly, the best I could get was encouragement from other autistic parents, unverified solutions from unverified sources, and low statistics of kids who eventually outgrow the spectrum - 40% or less. Days turned to weeks, weeks to months, and months to years; my son is seemingly regressing. Some days, he picks up a new and positive habit, and before you finish thanking God for the progress, he's completely stopped and picked up another not-so-positive one. At that point, you could only hope the new habit is not so long-lasting while praying for the best with the next. I started coming to terms with what the Therapist had told me: "You must let go of the child you thought you had so you can adequately love the one you have. Reality dawned on me. I was still angry, but I hoped things would get better this time.

3. Bargaining: Oh God, show me Mercy!

The Doctor's words kept replaying in my head "Favour has Autism with regressive tendencies."

This was too much for me to take. It was the hardest thing to accept but I was sure God would do something. I still remember in one of my devotionals, I took a copy of his reports, cancelled all the Doctor had written and by each statement (report), I wrote what I wanted to see. I had to strike a bargain with God. JB was 3 years+ by then and I made a bargain with God, "Father, I trust in you. Before JB turns 4, he'd have regained his speech and kicked Autism to the curb. In return, I will bring him up to serve you all his life."

I wrote that and placed it in my Bible and I had some calm. I placed my Faith on the line, I hoped and trusted God will not fail me this time around. I'll rather believe in God's mercy than in the Doctor's reports. I am a Christian and believe in God's word. I believe in the anointing of God upon His servants on earth but I don't run after churches, miracle promises and prophetic words. I have a place of fellowship; I have my Pastor. Whatever height I cannot attain Spiritually, I believe my Pastor will/can and that is enough for me. When you get desperate, you want to strike a bargain with just anything and everything. I will pray and beg God for mercy. "Oh Lord, show me mercy" sounds like what you've heard somewhere? Of course! This time around, I had to set an alarm just so I don't miss out on the viral early morning prayers. Anything to get JB back to being the awesome kid I knew.

4. **Depression: When hope is lost!**

I'm not the party type. I occasionally attend events and especially for Master of Ceremony functions. It was further compounded by JB's situation. I stopped taking him to places. I was embarrassed, ashamed and afraid of the stigma and gossip. I was more concerned about what people thought of my child than what he thinks of himself. I wasn't sure of how to react to his behaviour and tantrums in public. I secluded myself (him too) and could only attend Church services. I actually contemplated stopping Church at some point. He was busy living his life and I was busy hurting myself with my ignorance.I turned down many invites because of him (me actually). My ignorance and ego got the best of me.

Depression crept in. JB turned 4 and counting, yet, it looked like he's rather getting worse - the regression.

My prayers weren't answered. God didn't come through for me; He didn't show me MERCY, after all. The disappointment was real. I was so depressed, yet didn't know it. I recall during one of our therapy sessions, the therapist mentioned, she was concerned about my mental state. She had to assess my ability to take care of JB. She brought out a sheet of paper with questions which I was meant to answer from zero to five (zero being less likely while five was very likely). I did and scored five in all. She heaved and with this sad look on her face, she goes, "Delphine, I'm afraid, from the overall score you got, it shows you are highly depressed".

I'd heard about depression but wasn't really keen on it. Actually, I didn't know what it meant. She insisted I need therapy too and recommended I'm placed on antidepressant drugs. I immediately turned it down and promised, I'll be fine. Every symptom pointed to depression. I'd completely lost interest in activities, constantly tired, I lacked motivation and concentration (I was constantly lost in thoughts), I always caught myself crying and sobbing, I was in deep self-pity, I enjoyed isolation (id lock up myself indoors, stay in bed all day with no desire to wake up). I was constantly tired and suffered from insomnia. I felt inadequate being JB's mum; so inadequate. His dad was not with us and the burden was too much for one person to bear. I had no one to share my frustrations with and I'd so internalise my pain, I couldn't share with people - even those who truly cared. I thought they would end up judging me and calling me a bad mum. I wasn't sure who would understand me and who would use my pain as gossip news. Because most of what I'd prayed for didn't get answered, I lost hope! I lost hope in God, myself, my son, the system and in others.

5. **Acceptance: It is what it is!**

JB is now 5 and counting and still nothing. Same regressive tendencies. The mainstream schools started complaining. He wasn't coping with the setup - the stress on the teachers, the disturbance of the other kids, the constant calls for me to come pick him up and his inability to stay focused and learn. It was pointless! The school raised a complaint. Social Services got on his file and an EHCP (Educational Health Care Plan), done on every special needs kid to assess his capabilities and especially educational needs). It was drafted for him and at that point, it was obvious he needed a special needs school. A health care worker and special carer were equally put in place for him. It was already mid-term and amongst the schools available, Nexus Primary School was the only one with admissions still ongoing. Quite a distance from home but transportation was put in place to pick him up and drop him off. Every therapy session (Occupational, Speech and Language, Music) was reinstated.

I reluctantly accepted but there was a part in me that wanted help and rest from all the stress. Clearly, the government is doing the most to give my son the best he needs. Every provision to make the load light was made available. What else could I possibly ask for? Why am I insisting on staying in grief? "Delly, you'll have to let go of the child you thought you had so you can properly love and care for the one you have". I began accepting the fact that I have all I needed to overcome. I realised; I had more support than I'd initially envisaged. I was in such a privileged position; there are many out there who couldn't access this much support I have. I realised how ungrateful, impatient, illogical and selfish I'd been and how my actions contributed directly or indirectly to my pain and delayed the healing process.

My son is on the middle spectrum, you won't immediately tell he's autistic until you interact with him. He's the cutest child out there (his teacher describes him as the most handsome and confident black boy she knows). It could have been worse; others will give everything to trade places with him. I was so consumed with grief so much that I'd forgotten to count my many blessings. It dawned on me, I had put God in a box and was insisting on my own will rather than His. Miracles come in various shapes and sizes, different times and seasons. If it is not now, it will be later and until then, I'm willing to enjoy the process while it lasts. Whatever be the outcome, I was willing to accept my son in any condition and focus on being the best mom for him - Autism or not! I didn't just accept the situation, I equally repented and asked for his forgiveness. I held him, cried and repented from every wishful thinking. I promised him to be better and to give him the love deserving of a mother

THE HEALING!

It doesn't just suffice to accept the situation, there's a need to take corresponding actions. I became intentional at healing. I was willing to leave my comfort zone, discard my beliefs and myths, embrace my reality and find a way of making the journey easier and better for us. This means, I had to do some checks and balances, ask legit questions and get the right answers. I have to be OK with having a non-verbal kid that might never articulate like I do. I have to be willing to stand by him in good and challenging times without feeling embarrassed. I should be willing to deal with the fact that he has regressive tendencies and if anything positive comes from that, great! I have to be OK seeing him act below his age sometimes and most times. I have to be willing to make huge sacrifices with him being my priority. I have to be willing to come out and speak on Autism and share my journey so far with the community. I was OK with all these and I did!

I began taking him out. I was fine to watch him be at his lowest without feeling embarrassed or uncomfortable. Whenever I was called for my usual MC functions or mere invites and couldn't afford child care, I'd take him along while informing the celebrant of his condition. I began reading and researching even more. This time around, to educate myself on how best to love and support my son. I realised how unfair I'd been to him and how much time I'd lost on the wrong things. I realised I was too focused on those who were ignorant of his condition and missed out on those who were enlightened and more than willing to lend a hand.

I began making friends with other special mums and took keen interest in sharing ideas from my research. I was OK talking about his situation a lot more; sometimes, more than I should. I kept talking about Autism. I refused to sweep things under the rug anymore. I spoke about it as much as I needed to. I released all the pain, accepted the reality of things and I had to let everything out. The anger, the unspoken words, the thoughts, the pain, I had to release them all. I spoke about every thought that popped in my head, the good, the bad, the mundane ones, the love and the anger. I asked questions and got answers too. I spoke to myself in the mirror, I spoke to God, I spoke to my son and spoke to whoever cared to listen. I wanted healing and I was intentional at having it. Some days, I felt sad, lonely and angry again. It wasn't before I'd told someone or written about it in a diary - this book you are reading. It became a new hobby.

I let out the pain and was OK breaking down in tears even while talking. My confidence grew more and more and I could see instant changes in my son.

In Church, I let him be himself. I didn't always try to look over my shoulders (except, of course when necessary). JB's favourite place is Church - Royal City Mission London (My Family indeed!). He's sure to play the drums and/or keyboard whilst in Church. There's just something about the Church that keeps him "alive". He runs from pew to pulpit at will and couldn't care much about everyone else. He shouts when he feels like shouting, cries when he feels like crying, goes from one "favourite" of his to another. He's never bothered about you or anyone. You are probably the ones stressing over nothing. He's in this beautiful world of his and you either join him or watch him live his best life. I had enormous help from my Church Family; everyone willing to support me Morally, Financially, Mentally and otherwise. My acceptance of the entire situation was the missing piece needed to get everyone involved at their best.

I engaged in more physical activities with him, reduced his gadget hours, played more and laughed better. I noticed the spark he'd lost, returned. Eye contact was fully restored and before long, he understood finger pointing. He began eating more than he was doing (he'd completely lost appetite for especially African foods). We played more, related better, bonded more and healed even more.

Talk about school; JB loves school! He's excited to leave home every day 8am-4pm. No more crying when I'm taking him to his school car for his driver to take him to school. He's rather bidding me goodbye as he hops into the car. His driver thinks he's a good boy and well behaved. His teachers think he really loves school. He enjoys playing even with a few others. He learnt how to write, spell and read. Yes, he does! Though not fluently, he's such a great learner.

I started feeling the weight on my chest and shoulders lighten. Most things started falling in place. I could see my son had regained his spark and was more enthusiastic about life. I literally started living life again with my son - we were just existing. That was actually me "burying the child I'd lost" and embracing the one I'd gained. The height of therapy!

> *"Autism is not a processing error. It's a different operating system"*
> **[Sarah Hendrickx]**

CHAPTER 5:

DO'S AND DON'TS

"Meet your child where they are at, not where the world expects them to be."

[Jesse Evans]

A. PARENTS TO KIDS

1. Don't Communicate Poorly:

Of course, communication with special kids will require a bit more aptness and intentionality. The goal is to help them get at talking and interacting with others. Speech and Language therapy can make a big difference in helping them communicate more clearly, while occupational therapy helps them deal with things they feel through their senses and also gets their social skills up to speed. However, understand, you are your child's first Therapist. Every other is secondary. Meaning, there's a need for every parent to master the art of effective communication and sort out the best possible ways to improve on their child's communication and interaction.

- Always call them by their names or pet names so they are sure you're talking to them.
- Don't bombard them with long sentences. Keep it short and simple.
- Don't rush with your words. Pronounce them properly, if not, they might mistake it for other words.
- Maintain one language. Different languages will rather cause confusion and sensory overload.
- Don't pressure them for a response. Give them ample time to process whatever you're communicating.
- Maintain eye contact and use sign language to communicate better. Don't insist on communicating in noisy places.
- Don't reject other communication tools and apps. You can't do it on your own. With JB, I used Makaton & Pecs.
- Enrol them in Speech and Language Therapy.

2. **Don't Neglect Discipline:**

It can be hard to strike a healthy balance between Discipline and Abuse. Most times, in trying to show love and empathy to these kids, we tend to over pamper them. Of course, there are many reasons to justify why they get preferential treatment to the regular kids. However, parents must be careful not to blur the lines. Sparing the rod actually spoils the child; of course, not literal. Don't always let them have their way. Psychologists recommend, the most appropriate and effective way to Discipline them is by being assertive and authoritative yet kind and supportive, while encouraging them to be less dependent.

Generally, autistic kids thrive on routines and structures. Once that is properly established, they feel safe and trust sets in. Without which, they can hardly yield to order. Asking JB to perform whatever task will require the above, otherwise he'll never take you seriously. Oftentimes, I've had to stare at him intently while firmly giving him a task. He might reluctantly do it but with time, he has trusted me enough and feels safe to follow my lead. Other times, he's grounded from excess phone use, TV and games. He's learnt to follow instructions and order to get some favours. Discipline them right but don't punish them harshly by being too strict. Understand, these kids have enormous challenges and struggle with grasping lessons, especially the ones with regressive tendencies. It has been known of some parents who punish kids, shout at them, get them beaten and abused. This is punishable by law!

3. **Don't Compete or Compare:**

Don't compare your kid (s) with those of others or others; expecting them to act similarly or better. I cannot over emphasise on this. Quite often, there's this subtle competition that goes on in our minds about our kids with others. We compare parenting styles, intellect, physical attributes and even the spectrum. We expect them to reach milestones or react to therapy like the testimonies of others. If you ever read this book up to this stage (especially as a Special Parent) be reminded that I only shared my experience/journey to encourage and give you a pat on the back. My journey can inspire you but it should not make you want to replicate my experience or downplay your own unique journey. Remember every child is special and unique, presenting different spectrums with different exposures, talents and abilities. Fact remains, there will always be many special kids you'll come across doing far better than yours; be it in speech, talent or even in character and of course, there will be other

Special Kids you'll find in "worse" conditions than yours. Your job is not to compete, compare or contrast. As a Special Parent, focus on the responsibility God has entrusted you with; do the most you can and leave the rest. Comparing your child with other regular kids or other special kids is so unwise. Competition is the thief of joy. It breeds judgement, resentment and depression. I've trained my mind to immediately "kill and bury" such thoughts and stay positive, each time I've found myself in that competitive space.

4. **Don't Reject Help (Therapy):**

As someone taking care of them, remember it's super important to look after yourself too. While many don't understand your plight, others do and genuinely wish to support you. Don't hesitate to ask for it when needed and equally take it when it is available. It might be as little as a 30-minute break for a nap, a lift from the groceries back home, a gift voucher for some massage, a weekend away from the kid(s) while someone looks after them, etc. Don't reject professional help. Seek therapy too, for yourself. Ask assistance from the community, get ideas from other Parents, ask your kid's school for

73

extra support, join local support groups, research and read from experts. Whatever you do, get help!

5. **Don't Invalidate Their Feelings:**

Don't brush off or make light of their feelings and the tough stuff they face. Don't assume or think their reason for a meltdown is not reason enough. Sometimes, JB just starts crying over "nothing". He sobs for minutes and since he can barely speak, it gets quite frustrating as the reason for the tears is not immediately obvious; worse still, he rejects every attempt to calm him down. On the other hand, they might look indifferent and heartily express affection, but they certainly do! I randomly give JB a hug because he's always in need of it; whether to make him feel better or to appreciate his love for me. He needs it!

6. **Don't Violate Their Privacies:**

Most times, being the main decision makers for our kid(s), we tend to push the boundaries and forget they still have rights to their privacy. We forget, we are only custodians of them and should know when and where to draw the line. Quite hard for parents with non-verbal kids who really can't verbally express what they want or prefer.

This is social media dispensation where most persons see content in anything; even in the privacy of their kids. The desire to make money and the insensitivity to potentially damaging information. These kids are literally exposed regularly out of their wish by parents who clearly don't know their limits. You stand the risk of losing your kids to social services, thus should be careful what you share about your kids. What's the limit as far as your kid's privacy is concerned? It's as simple as what you won't share about yourself to the public. You don't share information about them without seeking their consent or at least the consent of the other parent, in a case where the child(ren) can't express themselves verbally. You can equally keep their privacies by teaching them personal boundaries; between strangers and family and equally the rights to not answer every question about them. JB has since been kept off social media for many reasons amongst which include, his privacy. His privacy entails you having privacy as well. You can't do just anything around them for whatever reason.

7. **Don't Act Unbecomingly:**

Again, these kids know better than you think. They understand beyond what you assume. They learn more from what they see you do than what you tell them. Actions speak louder, they say! Many special parents are known to be nonchalant in the midst of their kids, under the pretext, the kids don't understand or see them. If you're not proud of that thing, keep it away from them. JB will act like he didn't see or notice and you'll only notice the contrary when he's replicating the act. They are smarter than you think.

8. **The Glass Child Syndrome:** This is a family dynamic describing the challenges of growing up with a sibling who has special needs or a chronic ailment and often feel neglected, dismissed and invalidated because their parents have consciously or unconsciously invested their emotions, time, resources and energy in raising the sibling with medical needs. "Glass child" is from the idea of being too transparent (healthy enough) to be paid attention to. Many healthy children experience this and it somehow looks like they are paying for a crime they didn't commit. This usually has a toll on their

mental wellbeing leading to low self-esteem, isolation and even resentment of the special sibling. As a Special Parent, see to it that you strike a healthy balance; creating time for the "glass child(ren) just enough to make them feel as loved and cherished. Don't raise "glass children".

B. PARENT TO PARENT

1. **Don't Reject Co-Parenting:**

Healthy co-parenting is the best therapy for especially special kids. Parents, take note! Quite understandably, not every child is privileged to have both parents in their life at birth or as they grow; for various reasons. However, if you (as a parent) have the opportunity of having your partner around, kindly never deprive them of the other parent, even if you have sole custody. This is not a function of both parents being OK with each other. It is a matter of Principles. It took two to make these babies. It requires two to raise them.

The tendency of women (especially) using kids as a bait for scores settling with baby daddies/partners should be highly condemned. It was your choice for a partner. Understandably, your anger might be understood but not enough to deprive the kid(s) of their parents. The only justifiable reason why any parent should be denied access to their kids is in a case of sufficient evidence(s) of abuse. Otherwise, you'll be doing yourself and the kids, some injustice. On the other hand, there's been the tendency of the fathers becoming frustrated and abandoning the responsibility for the mums to shoulder by themselves. They are disappointed in how the child(ren) turned out and their own way of handling the situation is to blame the mum and abandon the child. This is as disheartening and selfish as it can get. Abandoning your responsibility to her only prolongs her pain/grief. She goes back and forth the different stages of healing and this is quite detrimental to the welfare of the child.

Again, whatever differences there are between you two, see to it that it has nothing to do with your kid(s). As difficult as this may sound, your children deserve this (healthy co-parenting) and you owe it to them. Worthy of note, men may express grief slightly differently from women. Their silence should not let you invalidate their pain. Oftentimes, they internalise their struggles, yet have to put up a facade for the family or public. Be emotionally intelligent enough to understand them at this point.

2. **Don't Downplay Emotional & Mental Support:**

Another thing co-parenting does is, it helps both parents with emotional and mental stability. It is more than just coming together for the kids. The mere present of your partner in the equation takes off too much weight on your shoulders. In my estimation, one special needs child is the equivalent of at least five regular children. That's how much work is involved. Imagine having to bear the entire burden alone. The difference between special parents with no mental and emotional support and those with adequate support, is immediately evident in the outcome of their parenting. In situations where one parent is unavoidably absent, do well to compensate for it from family, friends, therapy or even new relationships. Remember, you have to be emotionally and mentally stable to adequately and efficiently raise and instil the same values in your kids.

C. FAMILY MEMBERS & COMMUNITY

As a community, we are all a part of the spectrum; directly or indirectly. Family should constitute a really huge support system to such kids. If you happen to be a brother, sister, cousin, nice nephew, aunty, uncle to a child with autism, understand a lot is expected of you. Show the most love you can. If you are unrelated to them in any way; maybe never ever had an encounter with one, somehow, you will via a friend, neighbour, colleague or just randomly. It is important to understand the courtesy involved relating with them as a lot of errors are committed in this process. As a community, it is a collective responsibility to build a healthy environment for special kids; break the stereotypes, help them live their full potentials and kick autism to the curb. How?

1. **Be Emotionally Intelligent:**

These kids will not always act or sound as the regular kids. Matter of fact, they'll irritate you and get you worked up a little more than expected. They'll push your buttons beyond your limits. They might even be rude, mean and unfriendly. Hence, being the "big person" is a position you are expected to assume, always. Don't try matching their energy. You'll never win. At such times, you should exude more kindness, more empathy, more patience and tolerance. They need it!

2. **Lend a helping hand:**

Offer to help; don't wait to be asked or told. These persons are vulnerable; always requiring extra help even when it doesn't look like it. There's never a "hand" that is wasted. Don't feel inadequate and don't assume everything is OK. Your help can be one step short of someone getting into depression. Offer to stay with their kids for a day so the parents can take off and rest. Financial support is always a great idea, if you are religious, do pray for them, ask how to be of help and be kind with your words.

3. **Don't Judge:**

And before you claim to be non-judgemental, read further. Quite often, the world judges special kids and parents without knowing. You might not know you are judging but your words and actions will betray you. Africans especially, attribute all forms of disability to witchcraft, ill luck and carelessness. Asking a special parent if autism runs in their family, if they got their kids vaccinated, if they did something terrible in the past that could possibly be affecting them, if their blood groups matched their partner's, if they'll will have more kids, even going as far as telling them how they are meant to carry out their duties etc, is utterly insensitive and judgemental and it hurts, deeply. Your job is not to know the cause of their Autism. Your role is to help lighten the burden.

Other times, you judge them by your body language; frowning of the face, rolling of eyes, pursing of lips or outrightly moving away from them. Sadly, most parents of such kids' low-key feel judged and hurt but only a few will vocalise it. The most common of the judgements is via gossiping. You judge them when you gossip about your friend's kids with others; narrating awkward experiences you had with them, exposing their privacies with others, giving details of them to strangers, making assumptions and mockery of the situation. It doesn't get any worse than this. Be careful with your words. Again, they might just be one word short of getting someone into depression. Sadly, I've faced this first hand from some media persons and close friends; actually, one of the reasons why I've been intentional at keeping JB off the public up to this moment. Too many small-minded people out there who need a lot of schooling on this subject.

4. **Caution Your Kids:**

How we think and talk about ASD impacts how our children see them. I cannot lay enough emphasis on this! It is one thing to know how to deal with Special kids, yet another to extend the same grace and knowledge to your own kids. Most kids of this generation are overly vocal, curious and expressive. They however get insensitive as to where/when to draw the lines. Though drawn by genuine concerns and ignorance, it doesn't make the pain any less hurtful. I have this lady (mum of 4) I'd term, the most understanding mum ever. She's quite respectful and cultured. I have had the most encouragement and support from her, yet the most hurtful words from her kids.

I recall having a conversation with her kids and one of them goes "JB has zero IQ. He literally knows nothing". He said so while laughing and honestly thought he was just being honest (from his observations). I felt a sharp pain through my heart but I had to remind myself, he was only a curious kid, while calmly explaining to him that no child/ no one has a zero IQ. Only dead people have zero IQ since their brains are not functioning, I added. He seemed to have understood but went ahead and complained of the noise JB was making. "Please ask JB to stop the noise, it is so irritating", he continued. I kept my cool and purposed in my heart to keep educating this young lad as much as I could, while trying to calm JB down.

Guess what? It was on the motorway and I was driving. JB got uncomfortable because he's not used to sharing the back seat with many. I'd given them a lift and they were a lil noisy. Of course, JB was overwhelmed with the noise and started banging the car. That was his own way of expressing his frustrations. I understood him, they didn't.

Now, imagine another mum who had not healed from her grief and was still very sensitive to such words. I know the pain I felt at that moment but was Emotionally Intelligent enough to make excuses for these innocent kids. The situation would be different with other Special Parents.

Educate your kids on what Special Needs is all about and what is expected of them. Teach them to be more accommodating of the vulnerabilities of such kids. Teach them to exercise patience and be more empathetic and tolerant. Teach them that being silent is better than saying the wrong thing. Teach them to show support in words and action especially in times of a crisis. This is not just about the kids of others; it is also about dealing with siblings with Special Needs.

5. **Don't Make Assumptions:**

Be considerate enough to ask questions. Assumption is the mother of errors. Special parents go through more than you can imagine. One Special kid is the equivalence of at least four regular kids. Imagine the responsibility that comes along with that. This implies they might not always show up at functions due to lack of child care or the many emergencies that could arise. They might get appointments cancelled at the very last minute due to unforeseen circumstances. They might overreact or blow things out of proportion, occasionally get on and off depression etc.

Understand, their journey is quite daunting and the least you can do is show some understanding and extend some empathy. I've had people write me off and draw ridiculous conclusions simply because

I couldn't make it for their events and in response, drew ridiculous conclusions. Some will go as far as thinking "oh, she's too proud and thinks she's bigger. Sometimes, I've had to go out of my way just to meet their expectations and regret why I do so. Why? My efforts were not good enough. They expected more. They wouldn't understand. We all have a role to play, in kicking Autism to the curb, as in the words of Tyler Durdin, "I do not suffer from autism. I do suffer from the way you treat me".

CHAPTER 6:

CHALLENGES FACED BY AUTISTIC PARENTS

"Autism doesn't come with a manual. It comes with a parent who never gives up!"

[Kerry Magro]

A journey I never envisaged! One that I never would have wished for. No matter how much I explain, you'll hardly get it. Every day comes with its unique touch. You only pray to have a positive one and manage the negatives. My son is overly attached to me, actually, highly dependent on me. He wants me around even if I'm not in the same spot. He is OK with knowing I'm at home and in my room, even if we are not in the same room. He senses my absence the very next minute and throws tantrums till I'm back. I guess he's lived all his life with me; who else to trust and feel safe with? This translates to how daunting it is for me as a mum. Having to be his best friend, his spokesperson, his partner, his carer, his shoulder to lean on, his advocate, his first teacher and his mum.

It is overwhelming as you have to be at your best, for him to be at his best even when circumstances don't allow for such. You require at least six pairs of extra eyes and constantly have to look over your shoulders. One minute of eye closing, is one minute too many to have your world come crumbling. Sadly, he is not as emotionally intelligent to understand your feelings. Oh well, sometimes he does but can barely express it. Each time he sees me crying, he is indifferent and sometimes all he does is walk away; leaving me emotional and wondering what's going through his mind. It is not always as bad. We share great moments; moments I won't trade for anything. My son loves me so much; this I know! The warmth in my heart when I ask for a cuddle and actually get one. Sometimes, it only lasts a few seconds. Other times, he doesn't want to let go. It is the smile I see in his face when he sees me afar, coming towards him. It is how he hurries to get his shoes each time I'm about to leave home and the pain in his voice from a distance when I have to leave without him, then the deep heave of relief when he finally sees me back. The giggles when we play his favourite games and how he wraps his little hands around my waist when I'm taking him to his driver for school.

JB is non-verbal (has greatly improved though) so I've learned to understand his non-verbal communication.

There's this beauty of understanding him when no one does; when he's hungry or thirsty, when and why he feels uncomfortable around someone/something. That feeling of being the only one to hear his heartbeat, understand why he suddenly starts crying or throws a tantrum, knowing when he just wants to be left alone.

- **Potty Training:**

My oh my! I'd say, this literally is the most challenging of them all and till date, though 80% successful, the remaining 20% is still a nightmare. JB has been in nappies since birth till he was seven, I tried all I could and gave up. Potty training requires enormous patience and constant adjustments to their needs. Potty training has a lot to do with motor skills, effectively communicating one's needs and cognitive development. These are aspects Autistic people are not so good at which further compounds to the already very challenging exercise. One minute he seems interested and invested in the lessons (for whatever reason), the next he is just as confused. Potty training is easier managed and achievable whilst they are much younger. Once you miss it and they come of age, it is twice as hard.

I got tired of buying nappies as he became older. I bought him a chamber pot and he didn't figure it out. He'll cry and reject it. I resorted to using the toilet while having him stand by me. I'll literally do "number 2", show him and then flush it, just so he could retain the process. Awkward but what do I do? He still wasn't getting it. I started using a timer based on his routines. JB gets back from school every weekday at 4:30pm. I noticed he will do "numbers 1&2" immediately after an hour. I had to work something around that. I'll wait 50 mins after he gets home, untie his nappy and insist he sits on the toilet seat until he is pressed enough to pass out "number 2". I'll stand there and watch him so he doesn't jump off. JB will not! He was very uncomfortable with my presence and I resorted to standing outside to give him some privacy while hoping he'd get the message. He didn't. Sometimes, while I'm outside hoping he'll get it, he'll rather jump off the toilet seat, do number 2 on the floor and in a bid to clean up himself, smear the entire toilet walls with it. Yes, it was that bad. It was so challenging; I was constantly frustrated and lamenting but could not do much to help him. He kept on; will mess up himself, soil his nappy and didn't seem like he had plans of ever using the toilet by himself.

I read many articles and watched a couple of videos on potty training but all the lessons didn't seem to be working. I then invited the social worker who had to help me with a step-by-step approach towards getting the training JB needed. It wasn't easy. Like I mentioned earlier, JB has always been in nappies, without which he messes up everywhere. This time, I had to shut down my fear of watching him "smear number 2" on him or the walls a couple of times before he'll eventually adjust (if he will). I abruptly stopped the nappies (he'd just turned eight and it was getting increasingly difficult to manage his privacy while helping him out. First weeks and months were quite challenging. I stopped the nappy and had to monitor him. He kept on bringing the nappy to me as he wasn't used to dressing up without it. Sometimes, it took him up to three days to do "number 2" because he just didn't know how to cope without the nappy. I'll put him on the toilet seat, stay by the door sometimes for hours waiting for him to do the needful. He won't. Immediately he's all dressed up again, he does it on him.

JB couldn't understand why the change and sudden pressure. I was introducing something new (though not the first time) and it wasn't working because like you already know, they have an "insistence on sameness" thus, finding it difficult adapting to new routines. It was quite challenging and the thought of giving up will flash through my mind every minute. He kept on spending hours on the toilet seat doing nothing and the minute you put on his clothes, he immediately does "numbers 1&2". He had conditioned his mind to only use a nappy or his underwear. I couldn't really blame him as such. I kept on insisting. He gradually started learning. He initially started doing "number 1" in the toilet but will still do "number 2" in his pants. He would frequent the toilet every second just for a drop of urine and it became a routine. I was motivated and kept insisting on him doing number 2 in the toilet. He succeeded once and that was it. I celebrated with him and he could understand he'd done something positive.

As time unfolded, he got used to taking himself to the toilet, shutting the door after him and properly easing himself. However, his greatest challenge was at the level of cleaning up with a tissue. JB has poor motor skills; he can't hold the tissue paper well enough to clean himself. I bought flannels and wet tissues. He will abandon them and rather use his under-wears or any cloth he sets eyes on. Till this moment of writing, JB conveniently uses the toilet by himself, uses his underwear to clean up and then flushes. While awaiting the moment when he eventually gets to start using the tissue appropriately, I'm glad he can at least use the toilet and I've said goodbye to nappies. (Recommended YouTube videos: Poo goes to poo land)

- **Finding Love:**

    Most parents of Autists (the mums especially) face the most of society's stigma. It is quite difficult finding someone to love and even more difficult someone to stay in love. These are realities not often expressed but the effects are far reaching. Special Single Mums (Single dads too to a lesser extent) are known to channel the better part of their energy, time and resources on their kid(s), they want to love and be loved, they want to go out and catch some fun, they'll love to travel for vacation and only return when they want. They really don't have such luxury. Having a Special Child(ren) is as challenging as it gets and being a single parent will require at least twice as much effort.

Men approach them, they have crushes, they desire to be in relationships, they often fantasise about love and if they have their way, they'll have a loving family. No woman wants to single-handedly carry the load meant for two or many. Sadly, finding love is not always a strength they possess as they unconsciously send potential suitors away with their actions and reactions. They'll hardly find time to go on dates and even when they do, they can hardly focus. Most times, the dates are hijacked by conversations concerning their special kids and how demanding raising them could be. They want to hurry home because the nanny has to retire for the day. Their kid(s) comes first, second, third and forth before they factor others. Their countenance is greatly determined by that of their kids. Their entire lives are tied to taking care of these children.

How can you possibly blame them when they are usually "everything" to their kids? They play the role of Parents (Father and mother), best friend, first doctor, first therapist, first Priest, first teacher, mentor etc. Their brains are constantly working; looking out for these kids and in all these, they are expected to be in the best mental state, always. Without which, they risk losing their kids temporarily/permanently to social services. The thought of that inadvertently makes them see everything else as a distraction - even finding love. On the other hand, they have the stigma of society to face. Gossip mongers and take bearers who take pride in discrediting these parents in front of potential suitors. "Don't marry her, she has a history of ASD, he/she comes from a bad family, you can't cope with his/her children; they are ASD, are you sure you want to be associated with such ill luck"? These and many more are enough reasons why finding love could be a hassle.

- **Divorce:**

    According to Mary Carmel Wilson - a Senior Associate Solicitor at the Elisson Solicitors, *"87% of parents raising a child with a physical disability divorce. 80% of married couples raising a child with autism divorce, and the statistic is higher when there are multiple children with additional needs"*. Again, a conversation most couples rarely have. Most divorces begin the moment a diagnosis is given. The mental battle begins, with both parents questioning the lineage of each other. Quite often, they are not so open and honest enough to discuss their concerns and fears. They outrightly or silently blame and resent each other or will generally focus on pointing fingers at other secondary factors without addressing the root cause of their problem - ASD/special needs. Parenting can present numerous challenges and increase stress levels within a marriage ranging from emotional, financial, time management, consistent support and the overall pressure that comes with handling additional needs they were not mentally ready for. It is indeed challenging and only a few survive this (even the few who do, hardly get past surviving having another child(ren) on the spectrum). Before long, both parents get too stressed to be one another's support system and sadly, tend to solicit emotional support from others outside the marriage. This further compounds the already existing emotional gap between them. It is only a matter of time and divorce may be inevitable. In the case of partners who were not married (maybe just engaged or in a relationship), they hardly ever proceed to marriage. JB's dad and I have had our fair share of this. It took me these many years to come to the realisation of what the "elephant in the room" was.

- **Uncertainties of Having Another:**

    The chances of having another child with autism spectrum disorder (ASD) depend on several factors, including family history, birth order, and environmental factors. Note that if you have a child with ASD, the chances of having another child with ASD are about 20%. If your first two children have ASD, the chances increase to 32%. If you have a family history of mental health or neurological disorders, the chances of having a child with ASD may be higher. Now, you think about this. Many parents (single or together) silently battle the fear of bringing another child on the spectrum and if they suspect their partners, they'll secretly wish to not have more kids or would rather have them with other partners, accounting for the high divorce rates earlier mentioned.

    The challenges involved in raising these kids definitely accounts for this fear, given the uncertainties surrounding the causes of ASD. "What if I end up having more of them? What if the fault is from me? What if they turn out worse than the previous?" The "what ifs" are many. It takes the very courageous few to be open and share their thoughts, concerns, fears and desires. They want to be honest and not feel judged. I've had many parents come aboard my live-shows to share their experiences; amongst which, many have reoccurring ASD while some didn't. In a society where achievements are narrowly seen via marriage and kids, you don't want to be left out or castigated for having a different or slightly different mindset. You fear having more kids and equally fear what people will say not having more kids. Yet, you're left by yourself to face the consequences when/if they show up. I've often had to answer the question of "Mummy Delly, will you have more kids and when"? Oh well, I definitely do want more and I will. Just like others, the thought of having another is somehow scary but again, you won't be sure until you try. I believe so much in purpose. I believe in God's will for me. I pray I don't have another kid on the spectrum but I'll recklessly and graciously love them if they turn out just like JB.

- **Managing Emotions:**

Suppressing one's own emotions while managing a child's emotions is an art that should be added to every curriculum.

Special parents are known to be edgy quite often. They literally grief and often face anxiety and depression; emotions not properly expressed or addressed and before long, they are termed nagy, sadists, bitter etc. Most special parents (single mums especially) have only themselves to cry to. They tend to inadvertently transfer aggression on others, often moody, isolated, lonely and guilty. They will lock up and deprive themselves from socialising. People who will hardly understand your struggles and what it means having an autistic child, unfortunately have the most to say about you.

Dealing with emotional unintelligence from ignorant folks, societal pressures, labelling, the stigma and unfounded stories could be so overwhelming. Worse still, trying to communicate these emotions with the kids could be very frustrating as they are likely to not fully understand or respond like it is expected. I've had my fair share of the grief and just like I explained in chapter four, the healing process is usually prolonged by the ignorance of others. It took me realising that JB's wellbeing is fully dependent on my mental stability before I could bounce back; strong enough to face life.

- **Financial Burden and Limited Resources:**

Special Needs Kids in general don't come cheap. The demands are twice or thrice as hard and even more so as they advance in age. Apart from providing the usual needs expected for kids, Special Parents are expected to raise extra funds for medication, special childcare services, special foods which sometimes are unavailable locally, special schools and all the demands, therapy sessions and other recreational activities. Unfortunately, due to the very demanding nature of these kids, their parents can hardly pick up, be stable at or keep a job. They either face discrimination at the workplace or underperform themselves out of these jobs. This is typical in Africa where there are no government subsidies and funding to help such parents fund their bills. I'm fortunate enough to be based in a country that makes provision for my son's needs as he is considered a priority citizen. JB attends one of the best schools and has access to the best therapy sessions with extra social services at his beck and call. Imagine those in Cameroon or other African countries where such facilities are unavailable and parents sometimes have nothing or only a meagre salary to depend on.

- **Lack of Self-Care:**

Self-care is crucial for autism parents to maintain their physical, emotional, and mental health. As an autism parent, you must make self-care a priority. It is not selfish to take care of yourself; it is necessary to be the best parent you can be for your child. This can be achieved by simply taking breaks, exercising, eating healthily, practising mindfulness, building a support network, seeking professional help or taking advantage of respite services. However, this remains far-fetched to most Special Parents as taking breaks could be costing them their jobs since no employer has money to throw around with no job done. They will hardly even hire you knowing you have such challenges. Hence, the benefits option turns out to be the best bet. This however greatly limits one from the possibility of earning more and exploring more.

You'll end up breaking down if you don't find time to recreate and that will mean, your inability to take care of your kid(s). Remember, you have to be in the right frame of mind, best state of health and the best of emotions to appropriately take care of these kids. The fear of losing JB got me into self-care which I'm enjoying as it has established a healthy lifestyle and living till tomorrow.

In conclusion, taking care of yourself isn't a luxury but a necessity. When you are well-rested and less stressed, you're more capable of providing the best care for your child. To the rest of the world, be kind to special parents. They juggle emotional stress, financial struggles, and the constant pressure of balancing work and caregiving alone. A little kindness and understanding can make a big difference in easing their challenges.

Listen, the therapist needs a therapist too! As a Special Parent or carer, see to it that you are intentional about recreation. Most often, we want to be there for everyone and forget we need help too. TLC is not luxury! It is a basic necessity and you too are deserving of it. No one is ever awarded for being the most stressed. Consider stress management options like time for helpful self-talk, enjoyable family activities, organisation, relaxation exercises and self-compassion.

Get emotional support by connecting with other parents or carers who have autistic children, participate in social activities and in programs that help you understand your child's behaviours and develop strategies to support them. Don't reject help, have fun, prioritise yourself too and get support from many sources including, local support groups, charities, online courses etc.

> *"Autism is not a tragedy. Ignorance is a tragedy"*
> **[Kerry Magro]**

CHAPTER 7:

SIGNIFICANT PERSONS TO AUTISTIC CHILDREN

"I don't battle with Autism, which is simply my personality. I battle with people who don't consider what accommodations I need"

[Anne Hegerty]

Categorically, you cannot raise a special kid in isolation. It requires the collective effort of the community. The process is thrice as challenging (in my estimation) vis-a-vis regular kids. May I use this opportunity to appreciate these persons in JB's life who have made our journey as less demanding as possible. Without which, I'm not sure to boast of the self-care and mental stability I enjoy. Most of them came at the nick of time. It's thanks to them that we didn't reach a noticeable breaking point. Autists struggle quite a lot with social and communication difficulties, making it hard for them to relate with many. Their cycle is quite small and they have a world of their own. Many persons find it challenging relating with autistic persons due to the challenges faced interpreting non-verbal communication like body languages, facial expressions, voice tones, eye contact and hand gestures.

Understand, each kid/person on the autism spectrum will have their own autistic characteristics as well as a unique profile of experiences, personality and possibly other co-occurring diagnoses that are a part of what makes them unique. Hence, their experiences and relationships will vary. However, you'll have to get into their world or at least meet them halfway. Language also is usually a huge barrier for them and so, Autists will relate more with those who can communicate in a language they understand or at least understand non-verbal communication cues. Special kids have a very small but intentional world. They have intense interest and admiration for certain persons out of the ordinary. These people make them quite happy or just be themselves. They choose who they want as friend(s), relate with who they want to relate with and reject who they feel uncomfortable with. As a special parent, be keen on the choices they make and do not insist on imposing yours on them. Your favourites and "unfavourites" are not necessarily theirs and vice versa. Believe in their choices. Only then will they trust you enough to handle their inadequacies.

Having had my fair share of experience with Autists, I think it is safe to categorise their relationships in (but not limited to) the following: The Dads, The Favourites, The Disciplinarian, The Carer, The Therapist, The enemy, Social Gatherings.

- **The Dad:**

    Traditionally, mothers are the primary caretakers of autistic children. The overall role of dads in the lives of children cannot be overemphasised. Quite often, we ignore that role or downplay it with the presence of the mothers. It is important for both the child's mother and father to be involved in parent training whenever possible. However, I'd like to think there's a role meant for the fathers that no matter how much we twist it, it comes back to us with time. A father's role to an autistic son is to provide unwavering love, support, and understanding, acting as a strong advocate for his needs, actively engaging in his development, learning to communicate effectively with him, establishing consistent routines, and celebrating his unique abilities while navigating the challenges of autism, all while ensuring he feels safe and valued as an individual.

    The self-esteem of most kids is derived from their dads. It is therefore imperative for kids to have a strong bond with their fathers regardless of his relationship with their mums. Whether separated or together, see to it that there's that relationship with both parents. JB's Dad was not in the country when he was born. However, he has been present to the best of his ability. They have a unique relationship and their first ever meeting didn't feel like it was the first. They'd been boding virtually and in person which is crucial to the development and well-being of the JB.

Dear Philip Samson, You are a good father and forever, I'll appreciate you for this wonderful gift of motherhood. Thank you for all your sacrifices and for being the best dad for him. JB & I, sincerely appreciate you!

- **The Favourites:**

This is usually one or both parents or someone quite close to them who spends quality time with them. This particular person understands them quite well. The Favourite understands their non-verbal cues, responds accordingly, can tell when they are uncomfortable, knows what to do when they have a meltdown, is willing and available to give and receive hugs, knows and provides their favourite food and snacks, knows and provides their favourite toys, is willing to play and sing along with them, pampers them a little more than they should and lets them get away with most excesses. Of course, I'm JB's favourite. As his first teacher, first Doctor, first Therapist, first Priest, first Nanny, first Friend, spokesperson and the only available parent at the moment, it is only normal to be his favourite too. JB wouldn't mind if there were to be only one person in the whole world - his mummy. If you happen to find yourself in this position, you should understand most of what happens in their lives is highly determined by you - The Favourite. Be more intentional about their lives, their growth, transitions and general wellbeing.

- **The Disciplinarian:**

Quite often, we are unable to draw a line between being on the spectrum and what requires discipline. By discipline, I do not mean abuse. I'm about striking a healthy balance between what's necessary and what's out of place. To be firm enough and not allow them to have their way to their detriment. Most persons; parents and strangers will rather make excuses for their excesses, hence promoting destructive behaviour for fear of being judged or criticised for poor parenting.

The Favourites are good at making excuses and giving reasons why the appropriate discipline was not implemented. JB's Godfather has so far been best at playing this role. He is the sweetest uncle ever and most definitely knows best how to strike a balance between being an uncle and a Disciplinarian. He knows when to come with a huge bag of JB's favourite crisp and when to look him in the eyes and say STOP! JB automatically adjust when he sees his Godfather and the great thing about all of these is, JB is not afraid of him. He's rather alert and disciplined around him. The Disciplinarian gets the kids to do what the Favourites can't get them to do. Uncle Stanley gets JB to do the things I can't get him to do. It is the intentionality with which he goes about it. If JB has gone off track and suddenly sees or hears uncle Stanley from a distance, he immediately adjusts or completely stops whatever it was.

When JB goes visiting him, he walks in straight to his bedroom or kitchen without a second thought; more like "this is home". His wife says JB is their first son. That's how much bond they share. Again, JB is not afraid of him; he's understood his uncle enough to know he wants the best for him and clearly knows there's love in discipline.

Dear Stanley and Nadia, JB and I are grateful and we appreciate you for all you do! Special appreciation goes to other persons who have played significant roles worth showing gratitude. Thank you so much Uncle Emmanuel Siben, Uncle Didier Dimala, Uncle Lesley Abei, Uncle Patrice Tamo, Uncle Lavert Nchitu. Clearly, I would have stopped coming to church because of how demanding JB can be. You all however made sure that didn't happen. JB & I are grateful!

- **The Enemy:**

Autists/Special Kids have that one person they see as their worst nightmare. They'll do everything to send these "enemies" into oblivion. They detest their "enemies" with passion and feel these enemies are out to frustrate their lives. My Younger Sister who lives with us happens to be JB's number one "enemy". She is the one person I trust the most as far as JB's wellbeing is concerned. She is such a sweet soul; very harmless, yet, a no-nonsense person and won't tolerate JB's excesses for anything. She provides immense help which came handy after so many years. She's quite hardworking and sacrificial and when she came, she specifically told me she's here to help me out with JB. For almost a year, she took over the affairs of JB - school runs, feeding, potty training, personal care etc and because of that, my relationship with JB was a bit strained. JB has always been too clingy and wants his mum always. This time around, he had some restrictions and he wasn't finding it funny.

According to JB, his mum (mummy Delly) is the strongest person alive and of course, his greatest security. So, to see someone with so much guts to flaunt his mum's orders like his aunty, was definitely quite traumatising for him. Prior to her coming to London, I was alone with JB; been so since birth. JB was fond of having his way with most things. He wouldn't eat anything he didn't want to, nor would he drink anything he didn't want to. He was quite lean and was so fussy with food. Saying no was his default and he could go all day on an empty stomach. I am his Favourite and though I tried to be firm, he took me for granted. He'll reject food and insist on eating just yoghurt and crisps. Of course, he'll have his way, most times. All these ended the moment my sister came around. She curbed his excesses, forcing him to eat until he did.

JB had just one African food (Garri & okro) he was fond of eating. When Dilys came, she insisted on feeding JB with every kind of food and before long, JB began eating. Sometimes, my sister would spend hours insisting he eats and he'll eventually eat. JB was fond of perceiving the smell of food before rejecting it and if you insist, he'll hold food in his mouth only to later spit in the bin. All that stopped and JB left from being a fussy eater to eating with much appetite. Without exaggerating, there's hardly any food out there JB won't eat except for very reasonable circumstances. Food was not the only struggle, potty training, simple habits, courtesy gestures, etc.

JB experienced the peak of Echolalia; repeating (in anger) what my sister would say. He was always so frustrated seeing my sister around. When he gets back from school and meets my sister at home, he immediately gets to his room and locks himself up. If I dare leave home without taking him along, he'll cry his eyes out. He couldn't

113

share the same space with Dilys. If she's in the lounge, JB is in the room and vice versa. Up till this very moment, they are still playing cat and mouse at home. The enemy is very necessary to adjust their lifestyles, curb their excesses, get them doing what they'll hardly do with the favourites.

Darling sister of mine, words will fail me to express my gratitude. God has used you in many ways than you know. Thank you for making this journey less stressful. Remember when I held the shaving machine and he ran to you, held you tight and needed you to shield him from me? That was the most beautiful love scene I'd seen in a while. Never forget that episode. I know you know, JB loves you but expresses it differently. Thank you is not enough. I'll choose you for a sister in my next life.

- **The Carer:**

With her, everything goes! She has a job to keep, a reputation to protect, an organisation to protect and a special needs child to look after. He/she does all to be in the good books of both the parents and her organisation, even if it means displeasing herself. There is a line she can't cross. One wrong turn and the social services are after your entire

114

career with a potential *"life time sentence"*. They are aware of this and so, always alert. JB has had many of such carers but the most outstanding of them all - Yemi. She literally spoils him and JB takes her for granted! He knows she won't restrict him; at least not especially when he insists on something. Yemi is very meticulous with her job, has mastered the art of striking a healthy balance with discipline and love and you can tell she is not just about a salary. It is her sincere love for JB which is seen with how relaxed he is with her. With every other carer, JB will insist on having me around. It is however different with Yemi as JB is quick to tell me "bye bye" as soon as she's ready to take him out. I used to be edgy with the other carers and will stay anxious till they get back. With Yemi, I literally go to sleep.

Dear Yemi, I hope you get to read this and know how much gratitude is in my heart. You're a good woman and I'm glad to have had you in my son's life.

- **The Therapist:**

This would constitute either a professional set up or just that particular person that stimulates them mentally; reducing his meltdowns and making them laugh, play and learn. Figure out this person in your kid(s) life and encourage that relationship. Having regular visits to the Therapist might initially not seem like much is happening until you realise how focused they become and how therapeutic it is for them. JB naturally loves music and is quite gifted with the keyboard and drums. So, I figured a Music Therapy session will go a long way. I was right! He will stay on the keyboard and throw a tantrum when his session is over. He would not want to leave. In Church, he will stare at the drummer - Leslie Abei, in excitement and can't wait to hop on them when service is over. I guess he wants to be like him when he grows up. In Church, he will stare at Uncle Lesley Abei- the drummer, in excitement and can't wait to hop on them when service is over. I guess he wants to be like uncle Lesley when he grows up.

Dear uncle Les, you've been there in more than many ways. I will never take for granted the days when I had just you and aunty Nina to look after him. Your family embraced him and lent me a hand when I needed it most. JB and I are grateful!

- **The Intercessor:**

As a Christian we don't rely simply on Therapy and hard work. We pray! Sometimes, as JB's "prayer partner" and Priest, I get tired and exhausted. Other times, I lose my faith. Having someone stand in the gap for you in prayers is beyond words. Linda Brown - one of my sisters in church, reached out one afternoon and was like "Delly, can I have JB's date of birth. I feel led in my Spirit to pray for him. I can't tell you how that made me feel. Some gestures may look small but they go a long way. Thank you for strengthening my faith and interceding for JB when I didn't have the strength for it.

- **Social Gatherings:**

    Again, they want to go where they want to go. Quite often, Parents tend to isolate or restrict these kids from many social gatherings. Of course, that's the best way they understood protecting these children from the cruelty of the world. Social gatherings could be avenues for competition, ridicule and stigmatising. Hence, most special parents would rather seclude or isolate their kids than expose them to such cruelty. This is counterproductive as it prevents the kids from exploring the world and expressing themselves like they should. JB has three major places he looks forward to - Church, School and Park. Sunday mornings are his favourite. He's

DIARY OF A SPECIAL MUM

sure to spend time with his mummy and equally play the drums and keyboard after service. JB moves from pulpit to pew and while others are reciting scripture, he's busy looking for snacks to munch. He's so free and happy while in Church. This is very telling of the friendly and hospitable atmosphere the Church has.

Apart from Church, JB passionately loves school. He picks up his uniform early mornings on Saturdays or holidays hoping to go to school. You can tell school is another safe haven for him. The smile on his face when he gets back and the noise at home as he tries reciting some of his school work. He had been to other schools before Nexus Primary School and it was heart wrenching watching him melt down every morning as he approached the school gate. Then he moved to Nexus and I've since "gone to sleep". No random calls from school, no requests to pick him up before closing time, no crying, no worries. Rather, an institution dedicated to serving the vulnerable with love, tolerance, empathy and truth. Now, I see a handsome lad each morning, quite excited to go to school to learn and play. He comes home with ink all over his hands like "Mummy, I've been writing all day". It is the improvement in literally all aspects of his life and it gets better every day. Saturday is his favourite day of the week. JB is sure to be picked up by Yemi and taken to the Park. He loves it there and though he has severe social communication difficulties, he's beginning to struggle and play with the other kids at the park. When he gets back, you can clearly tell he has quite a fulfilled day.

- **Pastoral Care:**

To Rev Jesse Song for visiting me at the Lewisham Hospital Theatre to pray for safe delivery through a caesarean. During JB's dedication in Church, you declared that he will fulfil his God-given purpose, and writing this book may well be the beginning of that purpose. JB will grow up to be the "Song" that many will sing to kick autism to the curb.

"The best way to predict the future is to create it"
[Peter Drucker]

CHAPTER 8:

EXPLORING THE CONNECTION BETWEEN NUTRITION AND AUTISM

"People are fed by the FOOD industry which pays no attention to health and are treated by the HEALTH industry which pays no attention to FOOD!"

[Wendell Berry]

Disclaimer:

I'm no expert at this, and equally learning. 50% of the data on this chapter is obtained with permission from the Gold Star rehabilitation Centre and the Autism Parenting Magazine which I believe would go a long way.

Research has shown that nutrition can have a significant impact on individuals with autism. There is a direct and important connection between the brain and the gut known as the brain-gut axis. This basically means there is a two-way communication between the digestive system and the nervous system. Meaning, up to 70% of children with autism have impaired GI function. In turn, this directly affects brain function. Hence, the need to be selective with what your kids eat. While there are no specific foods or diets that can cure or treat autism, certain nutritional approaches may help alleviate some symptoms and support overall well-being

Most physicians do not recommend putting your ASD child on a special diet as there is no diet which is clinically proven to cure Autism. Restricting your child's diet may worsen the nutritional status of your child as they already show food preferences that leave very little room for variety in eating. Furthermore, these children are more likely to be picky eaters and prefer junk food, which is high in calories, carbohydrates, and sodium, with low nutritional value. However, certain dietary changes and nutritional interventions have been found to be beneficial. For instance, a gluten-free diet and a carbohydrate-free ketone diet have shown significant improvement in the behavior and cognitive skills of children with autism and ASD.

JB was a fussy eater but all that changed when his aunty joined us. When he started eating varieties, I was happy to finally watch him savour all kinds of food. Sadly, I wasn't too sure of his dietary needs as far as African foods are concerned.

The "Whiteman's" food however, is tricky especially given, it takes a while for most Africans abroad to adapt and fully understand the nutritional content of the foods. A lot of research ought to be done to get the appropriate diet even with their already limited options. However, I must underscore how daunting it is to stay consistent but if you remain disciplined, it will definitely go a long way. Plus, I'll advise you again to consult and confirm with a Dietician or Doctor before embarking on it.

FOODS TO CONSIDER - AUTISM FRIENDLY FOODS

When it comes to managing autism, it's essential to understand the role of diet. While studies indicate that diet does not directly address behavioural issues or other primary symptoms of autism, it is common for certain foods to potentially worsen a child's symptoms. While it is practically very difficult to stay off completely, it is logically ok to take in small portions. The goal is to improve the cognitive health of your child. Certain foods have been indicated to possibly impact gut health and behaviour in individuals with autism. These include but are not limited to: Dairy such as Cow's milk, cheese, yoghurt: contain casein, a protein some Autists are sensitive to. Dairy free diet may be helpful in solving gut issues.

- **Gluten-Free and Casein-Free Diet:**
   One of the more commonly adopted special diets for managing autism symptoms is a Gluten-

Free and Casein-Free (GFCF) diet. Gluten and Casein are proteins found in wheat and milk products, respectively. Some parents and caregivers have reported improvements in autism symptoms and related medical issues upon removing these proteins from their child's diet. This is the most difficult of them all as they (soy, corn and nuts, legumes, added Sugar: excess consumption of artificial, or added sugars, Processed foods: artificial ingredients, colours, sweeteners and preservatives) can have a negative toll on the gut health.

Vitamins and Minerals

Vitamins and mineral supplements are considered highly beneficial for children with autism and Autism Spectrum Disorder (ASD). These crucial nutrients can improve metabolic functioning and even reduce hyperactivity and tantrums. This is because certain vitamins and minerals play an important role in maintaining neurological health and promoting normal brain function.

To ensure a balanced diet, aim to include a variety of fruits and vegetables with different colors, as this can indicate a diverse range of nutrients. Encouraging children with autism to eat fruits and vegetables can be a challenge, but creative approaches such as smoothies, fruit kebabs, or vegetable dips can make these foods more appealing.

A balanced diet rich in a variety of fruits, vegetables, lean proteins, and whole grains can provide a broad range of these essential nutrients.

- **High-Quality Proteins**

Protein is an essential component of a balanced diet, and incorporating high-quality proteins into the meals of individuals with autism can provide the necessary amino acids for growth and development. Opt for lean sources of protein that are easily digestible and low in added preservatives. Here are some examples of autism-friendly proteins: Proteins can be included in various forms, such as grilled, baked, or steamed, based on individual preferences. Incorporating protein-rich foods into meals can help maintain stable blood sugar levels and promote sustained energy throughout the day.

- **Healthy Fats and Oils**

Including healthy fats and oils in the diet of individuals with autism can provide essential fatty acids, which are crucial for brain health and cognitive function. These fats also help with nutrient

125

absorption and can contribute to a feeling of satiety. Here are some examples of autism-friendly fats and oils: Omega-3 fatty acids are vital nutrients for brain function. They help to improve hyperactivity symptoms and reduce the risk of heart disease, depression, dementia, and autoimmune diseases. Eat oily fish, such as salmon, mackerel sardines, eggs, olive oil, and broccoli, at least twice a week, and seeds, such as flaxseeds (also called linseeds) and chia seeds, on most days. Fats and oils can be incorporated into meals through cooking, dressings, or as toppings for salads or dishes. It's important to prioritize healthy fats while minimizing the consumption of trans fund in processed and fried foods.

SEEDS

- **Chia Seeds** — Most kids have never heard of chia seeds, but they are a great addition to kids' diets for many reasons. In addition to being a great source of omega-3 fatty acids (the ALA type), chia seeds are high in fiber, antioxidants, and a variety of vitamins and minerals. Chia seeds can be sprinkled on salads, yogurt, or into shakes or smoothies. I like to add them to the energy bites my kids often eat for breakfast and snacks. They are also easily added to muffins, cookies, or almost any baked good recipe. If your child likes pudding then chia pudding is a great option as well!

- **Flaxseeds** — Flaxseeds are another food many children and teens aren't familiar with but are full of healthy fat, fiber, and various nutrients. They provide the ALA type of omega-3 fatty acids and can be easily incorporated into many foods. There are many crackers available that contain flaxseed, as well as some packaged pasta and bread. You can easily find ground flaxseed that can be added to shakes or smoothies, yogurt, granola, or baked goods. Mixing flax seeds with water also makes a great egg substitute in recipes!

FOODS TO LIMIT OR AVOID

While focusing on autism-friendly foods, it's equally important to be aware of certain foods that may have a negative impact on individuals with autism. Here are some food categories that are commonly recommended to be limited or avoided in an autism-friendly diet.

- **Artificial Additives and Preservatives**
  Artificial additives and preservatives, such as food colourings, flavour enhancers, and artificial

sweeteners, are often found in processed foods. These additives have been associated with hyperactivity and behavioural changes in some individuals, including those with autism. It is advisable to read food labels carefully and choose products that are free from artificial additives and preservatives whenever possible.

- **Gluten and Casein**

Gluten and casein are proteins found in wheat and dairy products, respectively. Some individuals with autism may have sensitivities or intolerances to these proteins. While research regarding the effects of eliminating gluten and casein from the diet is still ongoing, many parents and caregivers have reported improvements in behaviour and digestive issues when their child follows a gluten-free and casein-free diet.

- **High Sugar and Processed Foods**

High sugar and processed foods should be limited in an autism-friendly diet. Excessive consumption of sugary foods and beverages can contribute to energy imbalances, affect mood stability, and potentially worsen hyperactivity. Processed foods, such as packaged snacks and fast food, often contain high levels of unhealthy fats, added sugars, and artificial ingredients. Instead, opting for whole foods and homemade meals can provide better nutrition and support overall well-being.

It is important to note that each individual with autism may have unique dietary needs and sensitivities. Working with a healthcare professional or registered dietitian who specializes in autism nutrition can provide personalized guidance and help determine which foods to limit or avoid based on the specific needs of the individual. By being mindful of these food categories and making informed choices, parents and caregivers can create an autism-friendly diet that supports their child's overall health and well-being.

BUILDING A BALANCED AUTISM FRIENDLY DIET

When it comes to creating an autism-friendly diet, building a balanced and nutritious meal plan is essential. By incorporating the right foods in the right quantities, you can support the overall health and well-being of individuals with autism. Here are some meal planning tips, along with strategies for incorporating variety and colour, and the importance of hydration.

129

MEAL PLANNING TIPS

Meal planning can simplify the process of providing nutritious meals for individuals with autism. Here are some tips to consider when planning meals:

⇒ **Create a schedule**: Establishing a routine and sticking to regular mealtimes can help individuals with autism feel more secure and comfortable.

⇒ **Involve the individual**: If possible, involve the individual in the meal planning process. This can help increase their engagement and willingness to try new foods.

⇒ **Be mindful of preferences**: Take note of the individual's food preferences and dislikes. Incorporate their favourite foods into the meal plan while gradually introducing new options.

⇒ **Plan for sensory sensitivities**: Individuals with autism may have sensory sensitivities that affect their food choices. Consider the texture, temperature, and visual appeal of the foods when planning meals.

⇒ **Incorporating Variety and Colour:** Aim to include a diverse range of foods in the autism-friendly diet to ensure a wide spectrum of nutrients. Here are some strategies for incorporating variety and colour:

⇒ **Fruits and vegetables**: Include a colourful array of fruits and vegetables in the diet. These nutrient-dense foods provide vitamins, minerals, and antioxidants essential for overall health.

⇒ **Whole grains**: Incorporate whole grains like quinoa, brown rice, and gluten-free oats to provide fibre and essential nutrients.

⇒ **Proteins**: Include high-quality proteins such as lean meats, poultry, fish, eggs, legumes, and dairy products (if tolerated). These proteins supply essential amino acids for growth and development.

⇒ **Healthy fats**: Include sources of healthy fats like avocados, nuts, seeds, and olive oil. These fats provide energy and support brain function.

• **Importance of Hydration**

Proper hydration is crucial for individuals with autism. Here are some tips to ensure adequate hydration:

⇒ **Water**: Encourage regular water intake throughout the day. Offer water during meals and between meals to prevent dehydration. Keep water in a very accessible location and remember they usually like a particular cup.

⇒ **Limit sugary beverages**: Minimize the consumption of sugary drinks, as they can contribute to excessive calorie intake and potential health issues.

⇒ **Infused water and herbal teas**: Consider offering infused water with fresh fruits or herbal teas for added flavor and variety.

By following these meal planning tips, incorporating a variety of colorful foods, and emphasizing the importance of hydration, you can create a well-rounded and balanced autism-friendly diet. Remember to consult with a healthcare professional or a registered dietitian experienced in working with individuals with autism to ensure that the dietary needs of the individual are met.

TIPS FOR PICKY EATERS

When it comes to children with autism who are picky eaters, introducing new foods and ensuring a balanced diet can be a challenge. Here are some helpful tips to make mealtime more enjoyable and nutritious for your child

INTRODUCING NEW FOODS

Introducing new foods to a picky eater with autism can be a gradual process. Here are a few strategies to try:

- **Start small**: Begin by introducing small portions of new foods alongside familiar foods. This allows your child to become more comfortable with the new food without feeling overwhelmed.

- **Offer choices**: Give your child a sense of control by offering a selection of healthy foods for them to choose from. This can help them feel more involved and willing to try new things.

- **Food play**: Engage your child in sensory play with new foods. Encourage them to touch, smell, and explore the food before attempting to eat it. This can help reduce any anxiety or aversions they may have. Remember to be patient and persistent. It may take multiple attempts before your child is willing to try a new food. Celebrate small victories and provide positive reinforcement to encourage their progress.

Sensory-Friendly Mealtime Strategies

Many children with autism have sensory sensitivities that can impact their eating habits. To create a more sensory-friendly mealtime environment, consider the following:

⇒ **Texture and temperature**: Pay attention to the textures and temperatures of the foods your child prefers. Gradually introduce new foods with similar textures to help them adjust.

⇒ **Visual appeal**: Presenting food in an appealing manner can make it more enticing for your child. Use colourful plates and arrange the food in visually appealing ways to make the meal more inviting.

⇒ **Sensory breaks**: Allow for sensory breaks during mealtime if your child becomes overwhelmed. This can help them regulate their sensory input and reduce anxiety.

By creating a calm and supportive environment, mealtime can become a more positive experience for your child.

TIPS TO HELP ALONG THE WAY

Adjusting to a new diet or trying new foods may be difficult for those on the autism spectrum, especially if they experience food aversions. Here are a few tips to help make the transition as easy as possible:

⇒ **Consider your child's current preferred foods**. Consider what texture, colour, or temperature their foods are. Consider offering new foods that are similar to their favourite foods to help them feel more at ease.

⇒ **Remember that "eating" is not the only food win!** Having a new food on the plate, touching it with a fork, smelling it, and even chewing and spitting are all great wins! Taking it one step at a time will help it feel less overwhelming. Also keep in mind that autistic children and adolescents can take longer to adjust to dietary intervention.

⇒ **Don't force a child** to eat food before they're ready or remove their favourite foods in an attempt for them to eat healthier foods "when they are hungry." Sensory issues do not resolve with hunger and this approach may cause more harm than good.

⇒ **Work alongside a dietitian** who specializes in autism to help provide accountability and creative ways to expand your child's diet. Stay in touch with your healthcare provider or dietician during the process of introducing new foods in case the new meals cause gastrointestinal issues or other behaviour-related changes. Only you, your child, and a healthcare provider or dietician can decide what diet is right for your child's dietary needs. Be sure to talk to a healthcare professional about your diet before making any changes.

FAQs

Is there a specific diet that can cure autism? No, there is no one diet that can cure autism. However, studies have shown that dietary changes can help manage symptoms and improve overall health.

Can a gluten-free, casein-free diet really help people with autism? While not everyone with autism will benefit from a gluten-free, casein-free diet, some studies have suggested that it may improve behavior and cognitive function in some individuals.

Are there any supplements that can help manage symptoms of autism? Some supplements, such as omega-3 fatty acids and probiotics, have been shown to be beneficial for people with autism. However, it's important to talk to your healthcare provider before starting any new supplement regimen.

Can food allergies or sensitivities worsen symptoms of autism? Yes, food allergies or sensitivities can contribute to inflammation and worsen symptoms in some people with autism. It's important to identify and avoid any foods that may trigger an allergic reaction or sensitivity.

CHAPTER 9:

THE ADVENTURES OF JB
EMBARRASSING MOMENTS WITH JB

"Autism is not a death sentence, it is an adventure".
[Delly Singah]

Vicarious embarrassments are worth sharing.
Being a social emotion, which isolates the victim based on
stereotypes, I decided to use it to promote the education of
it. The goal is to get many people to leave their habitat of
ignorance. Oh well, looking back, it never used to be so. I've
had my fair share of fighting these moments. Some days, I
wanted the ground to open and swallow me up, other days, I
couldn't hold back the tears, while some, I wanted to act
stupid for once. My ego was at play. I was more conscious
of my environment, status as a Public Figure and the "what-
will-people-say" conundrum. I sort after perfection and
would force JB to be all of what he could not. I'll amplify his
strengths and make excuses for his excesses. I wanted the
world to perceive him in a different way - the wrong way. I
was ashamed and embarrassed when he was himself and
would constantly shout at him and was quick to stop him

from doing anything that was potentially embarrassing. I was selfish! Then I grew up, became the mother I was meant to be and "buried the illusion" in my head. I realised, it is only embarrassing because I powered it and made it so! My ego was too huge, I had to crush it. If you truly care about your child(ren), your first impulse to such "embarrassing" moments would be "is my baby OK? Did my baby hurt himself? Is my reaction to the situation causing more harm or good?

When I learnt to prioritise JB's wellbeing; making him my top priority (I owe him that), I started seeing such "embarrassing" moments as learning curves in our journey and to a lesser extent, an opportunity to laugh out loud over his adventures. Yes, he is only being adventurous. Now I share this so you too can relate and feel less alone; no shame, no embarrassments.

1. **My first major encounter with the police:**

JB was just about five years old. It was barely two days after we had just moved into a temporary accommodation and still trying to understand this setup which was quite different from the rest of the accommodations we had lived in. Unlike the others, this particular one was shared with many others (more like a dormitory). Sad part of this was the bathrooms and toilets were external - shared and detached from the rooms. You had to walk for a minute or less to shower or toilet. Plus, this building was alongside the road at 40MPH. On this fateful day (day 2 of our stay in the property), I had taken him to the bathroom and forgot some toiletries. Careless enough, I left him in the bathtub and rushed to get the toiletries. Now, believe you me, I didn't spend up to a minute in the room. I knew where the items were and I only had to grab them and return. Lo and behold, I returned to find an empty bathtub. Clearly, he left the moment I did but instead of coming after me, he took to the back door which was always unlocked (though closed) as it was used by many. No, he didn't stay outside the building. He walked to a nearby pub, completely unclad and barefooted. Yeah, you read that right. Imagine the confusion when I returned to find an empty bathtub. I couldn't for a second think he'd left the building. My guess was, "keep looking round, he must be within and nearby. I quickly climbed upstairs, started knocking on doors. Most of the housemates didn't recognise me as we had just moved in. However, this had to do with a five-year-old and they were all alarmed.

139

Seconds turned to minutes and more minutes. I started panicking. My mind flashed on everything negative - "a bad neighbour high on drugs had kidnapped him (there was a stench of weed from the corridors), he had been stolen by some lady, just every negative thought". I rushed back to my room, nothing. The thought of him being outside crossed my mind but I immediately rejected it. Well, I went outside, rushed to the road and couldn't find him. I became scared and more confused. I could barely explain what happened to anyone. Everyone was worried and one of the concerned ladies proposed I call the police at that stage. I was worried but had no choice. I called and after all the necessary questions, I was asked to calm down and that there's a boy in their custody that matches my description and immediately gave the address. Lord, the sigh of relief! My next concern, "will the Social Services take him away?" They had every right to do so. I had messed up. I hurried to the location they'd given me. Yes, it was him, now clad in a skirt and blouse, eating crisps and looking like a cute little girl. I held my laughter. That was the most the bartender could do - her best was good enough. As JB lifted his head and saw me, I saw his face lit up with his usual angelic smile and quickly walked towards me. Everyone burst out laughing; even the policemen. The Pub lady was busy serving drinks when a small man in his "birthday suit" walked in confidently. "That was the most terrifying thing I'd ever seen", she added. "I immediately tried questioning him "Hello, where is Mum? What's your name?". No response, so she immediately alerted the police. We were accompanied back home by the police; they did the necessary checks to be sure if my version was right and the rest is history. Rather than being embarrassed, I could only thank God for keeping him safe; social services didn't take him away.

2. **JB grabs phone from a man's back pocket:**

I took JB shopping at the Blue Water Shopping Centre - London. I bought many things and had to struggle a lot as I pushed him in his buggy. It was a long day and He was definitely overwhelmed and started having a meltdown. He wouldn't let me do anything. He became inconsolable. I assumed he was hungry so I stopped at *McDonalds* to get something he could eat. He was very fussy with food but that was all I could think of using to calm him down. My phone was off and I had no charger. We got to McDonald's and met with a really long queue. His tantrums got worse. He didn't quite understand why we had to wait. There was a certain tall gentleman in front of us. He had his phone, visibly showing at the back of his pocket. JB didn't waste a split second to pull it off and immediately sat on the floor and struggled to browse. The shock in the guy's face, the speed with which he turned around, the force with which he grabbed JB's hand to seize his phone. He was so angry and wouldn't listen to my plea of "I'm so sorry. He's autistic". He gave me the look of "I know you sent him to *nick* my phone". He had this rude demeanour and as if he'd punch me in the face if no one was watching. JB got to his lowest. He had completely lost it and was screaming at the top of his voice. Imagine the crowd at the mall; all eyes on us. I was embarrassed to the point of no return. I had to focus on JB and find a way to calm him down; ignoring everyone else. He didn't stop till we got home. The stress of that day still remains indescribable. I wept! I cried in pain and in sorrow. I literally threw a pity party and "feasted". Well, night came, day also came. Today is here and the rest is history.

3. Wig in the wind:

Back in the days when I was still a fan of wigs. I had one on and had taken JB somewhere. I wasn't driving yet so we chartered a bus. Whilst at the bus stop, JB became anxious. We had waited for our bus for more than an hour to no avail. Other buses going to various destinations would alight at our bus stop and JB would pull my hand towards the bus hoping we would hop on. After so many buses went by, he couldn't take it. He began pulling me and crying. He couldn't understand why I insisted on staying there when we clearly had options. Suddenly, he got hold of my wig and started pulling. His grip was so firm, I couldn't overpower him. My wig was coming off, and the passers-by were watching and laughing. Some stifled, others triggered while some chuckled. "Lord, this wig had better stay on my head. I obviously don't trust the "bakala" (cornrows) underneath. I had to protect my integrity at all costs. "There is no way I am letting these people see the dandruff under this wig". Again, the thought of punching him in the face just to have my way flash

143

through my mind. I was still holding on but the wig was like 90% off already. JB held on and kept pulling. I realised his safety was more important than my "reputation". I let go. He threw the wig on the ground and held my hand pulling me towards an oncoming bus. Imagine the embarrassment of picking up my wig and it was pointless wearing it again. Lo and behold, the long-awaited bus arrived. The speed with which I jumped on board and couldn't afford to look outside through the windows as I could still feel the eyes of everyone on us. The relief in JBs face, still holding onto me, with the look of "I love you mummy. Let's go home". The bus drove off and the rest is history.

4. **Eating with an uninvited guest:**

I once had a speaking engagement in a different town and had to take him along as I didn't succeed in getting a Minder. I'd informed the celebrant who accepted that I could come along with him. Public transport is quite a challenge with them but I had no choice as I wasn't driving yet. We got on the train and I intentionally picked a seat away from others, as the train wasn't crowded. I'd factored all his excesses and literally just wanted to be far from drama. The train took off and after a while, this white Dude hops on with his daughter (I presumed), just about JB's age. They sat adjacent to us but were like three meters away. After a few minutes, I noticed JB started fidgeting. Apparently, he had seen this little girl eating his favourite crisp. He wanted it but since he's non-verbal, he couldn't express that need. I sat in a way that prevented him from leaving his seat. Suddenly, I realised Jesus boy (with his usual speed), forced himself under the locker-table and the next thing, he was with this white young lady sharing her bag of crisps. Matter of fact, before I could even stop him, he'd grabbed the entire pack and was returning to his seat. The shock on the young girl's face with teary eyes. Apparently, the girl's dad immediately understood he was dealing with a special needs child and even when I tried excusing the mess, he kept assuring me not to worry and that he fully understands. He was so kind, polite and understanding. He turned towards his daughter and pleaded with her to understand. I saw genuine understanding from a total stranger. He was willing to temporarily sacrifice his daughter's happiness to calm down a situation. JB had no business with

145

whatever it was we were talking about. All he knew was, he was craving for crisps, he saw crisps, he took it and now he's eating it. I embarrassingly walked to my seat and couldn't even lift up my head to the end of the journey while JB kept on munching his crisps.

5. **Hurtful tiny fingers:**

This faithful Saturday evening, I'm making dinner while JB in his usual manner is jumping all over. He is quite fond of me and can hardly spend 3 minutes without checking on me. I guess I'm his safe haven. I use a flameless cooker and I'd just taken the pot off the burner and was washing dishes in the sink when suddenly I heard a loud cry from JB. I immediately panicked because that was literally the loudest I've heard him since birth. JB has a low pain threshold and barely knows how to cry out loud like other kids. He struggles to express pain and most often, he just sobs and gets watery eyes, even if the pain is real. This time, I could tell it was excruciating, I guess the most he's ever felt. JB touched the burner and "fried" his fingers. He immediately ran into his room. That's typical of him. He'll rather hide it just so I do not get to tamper with it. I immediately ran after him asking what the matter was. He kept on hiding the particular hand to his back. I could tell something was wrong but couldn't pinpoint it. I insisted, grabbed the hand and what I saw, matched the pain he'd expressed earlier on. In that scenario, I'm meant to run it under cold water for at least 20 minutes before applying anything on it. JB wouldn't let me come close to him; much less touch the hand. It was all swollen and filled with water. I called **999** and was asked to rush him to the hospital which I did. Imagine driving with a crying baby in pain. The danger in all that. Guess what? During that entire time, he's busy bursting and peeling off the swollen fingers. We got to the hospital and it was a hassle getting a Doctor to see the hand in question. JB won't let anyone come close. After much struggle and screaming, the hand was disinfected and he was given some painkillers which he spat on the floor and like a waste of my entire time, I drove him back home and the rest is history.

6. **Check the closest groceries shop:**

After Church on a certain Sunday, everyone is busy greeting one another. JB loves the drums so I let him play them for a while before taking him home. Most of my Church members already know he's on the spectrum and have tried to factor in his needs. Few of them keep an extra eye on him as they already know how swift and adventurous he can be. I'm busy greeting Church folks and thinking he's playing the drums when suddenly, I couldn't find him. Our Church is directly opposite TESCO (one of UK's top groceries shops), separated by a busy road. While everyone started panicking, I was calm. I could only think of one possible place - TESCO. I tried stopping him from having his favourite crisps and didn't provide any alternative. Of course, he knows his way around and doesn't need anyone's permission. In JB's world, his mum is a shareholder of every grocery shop in the UK and he's allowed to eat and drink whatever he likes, when he wants. I rushed there and of course he's there, has opened an entire bag of crisps containing 30 mini packs of crisps, sits on the floor and is busy munching. The store manager and security guard tried engaging him in a conversation which he went mute and kept eating. He only lifted up his head and smiled when he saw me. I apologised to them and even before explaining his condition to them, they had

DIARY OF A SPECIAL MUM

understood. I gave my contact and pointed to my Church; in case he returns another day. He sure will.

7. **Door of a moving car opens:**

I'm driving on a highway and had JB in the back seat. I had just started driving so, you can imagine how focused I'm meant to be with the steering. Suddenly, I noticed a breeze in the car and when I peeped via the mirror, JB, in his usual play mode, was touching the door and found a way to open it. As far as I know, the kids lock was on and the door locked. I was wrong, it was closed but not locked. I screamed at the top of my voice, I panicked and without thinking nor looking, slowed down and was trying to manage the situation. Now if you're a good driver, you'll understand that was a potentially catastrophic accident scene. I could literally hear the driver behind holding a sharp stop on his brakes to stop his car from bumping into mine. Other cars kept honking and the more I got confused. I received all sorts of insults; the "F" word almost went into extinction. I succeeded in turning on my hazard lights, indicated parking on the hard shoulder, went out and got the door locked. I was literally shaking and shedding tears whilst JB was quite in oblivion of

149

what had just happened; so unperturbed. I got in and drove off and each time I flash back to that episode, I'm still frightened.

8. **First flight, first trip, first visit to Africa:**

Of course, travelling to Cameroon for the first time in 8 years was definitely not going to be a walk-to-the-park. I didn't have enough money for a business class ticket so we got economy; we shared our seats with another guy who sat by the window. I took the middle seat while JB was next to the aisle. Being JB's first travel and flight experience, he was quite unsettled. Recall, he occasionally struggles with sensory overload and particularly has a phobia for crying children (noise sensitivity). We took off and he was calm for some minutes. Suddenly, this baby in the middle column started crying and wouldn't stop. JB was so uncomfortable and since he is quite small, his seatbelt was not so firm. As the child kept crying, JB couldn't take it anymore and with his usual speed, pulled off his seatbelt, and before I knew it, he was already close to the baby, trying to stop him from crying. Now, understand JB is not violent. He was only distressed and uncomfortable. All he wanted was for the baby to stop crying so he could focus and because JB is non-verbal, he turns to act impulsively. He reached out to stop the child, grabbed the dad's shirt and kept pulling as the baby's dad was preventing JB from reaching the child. I stood there confused, struggling to pull him off the shirt. I did and pleaded with this very furious guy to understand. He could tell JB was special needs and though still furious, he calmly requested i get a business ticket for next time. He was right, JB shouldn't travel economy for his comfort and for the safety and comfort of others too.

9. **Visa stamped on every passport page:**

I had a conference in Cameroon organised by the ICT-UNIVERSITY and this time, I was going alone. The relief of knowing the huddles of last trip were not happening again; at least not yet. Parked my stuff and headed for Heathrow - Airport. Actually arrived 2 hours earlier for my flight and made sure I had enough time to relax. Gkt to check in and had to present my passport. Boom! JB had written on literally every single page. He made sure he drew himself in some of the pages, wrote a love letter to his mummy in others and stamped a visa to every country in the world. More like mummy, travel the world, it's your time! No more visa refusals. That's the only explanation I could give to spare myself the embarrassment in front of me. Two weeks prior, I'd checked on my documents to be sure all was intact and since I was about to travel, I had to remove my passport from the safe and together with other documents, placed them in the bag I was to use as my hand luggage. JB got hold of it and the rest is history. This lady took my passport and couldn't believe what she was seeing. Interestingly, he didn't write on the information page so all my relevant information was showing. She made a few calls and I was only allowed to travel because my details were still showing. I made a successful trip to Cameroon and as silly as I was, I assumed, it will be the same understanding with the Cameroon immigration coming back. Finished my conference, travelled down to Douala for my return flight. Got to check in and only then did I realise I was no longer in the UK. I was told I can't travel and that my document is invalid. I cried my eyes out, begged and still didn't say yes. I mean, the airport authorities were right, who travels with such a passport? My flight got cancelled and I had to travel back to Yaounde for a new passport. The stress, the expenditures, the risk, the tears. Long story short, I made the passport and returned to London. Got home and the innocence and smile on his face when he saw me was enough to melt even the stoniest heart. I love him, recklessly.

10. Extras:

Now, this bid is not exactly an adventure of JB, it was more of an unfair treatment I got at the Douala International Airport - August 2023. I documented this on my Facebook page titled "Cameroon my country, not as bad after all part 5 & 6". I had to share it (copy, slight editing and paste) here because, of course, it remains my most frustrating and embarrassing encounter with an insensitive human on Autism.

My son and I landed at the Douala International Airport and because he is British, he needed a Cameroon visa. I'd procured one for him already but it was still in e-visa format. This meant a stamped visa in his passport was needed upon arrival. This is due process for all foreigners. First check point was a Police officer. I presented the e-visa on my phone and crossed with no stress. Next check point was to fill out an arrival form. I remember asking a lady (in uniform) if I was meant to fill it up, she said No! The confusion was "she assumed I am a foreigner even though she saw my Cameroonian passport, I guess) and said I should go to the next Kiosk. I'm not 100% sure why she said I should go to the next stage. Well, I guess, God wanted it so. I was rather meant to fill two forms, stamp my son's visa before going to the finger print Kiosk. I ignorantly skipped the queue and rather went to the last stage of checking out. My, oh my!

Then comes the famous Jezebel (I have her complete name as it was boldly printed on her uniform but this is how I choose to describe her attitude towards me). There was a guy standing in front of me, waiting to be served. We were on the same flight and he sat next to me and saw how challenging it was with my son. So, he opted to assist me with my hand luggage. He was being served so I was directly behind him, whilst holding firm to JB's hand so he doesn't wander off. He was so tired and couldn't bear standing in a queue. This guy finished and it was my turn. I gave a smile to this lady and she didn't reciprocate. I knew immediately she was a hard nut. She asked in French "Madame, *Où sont vos formulaires complétés?* (Madam, where are your completed forms?). I was told I did not need one. Trying to explain how the other lady misled me, she immediately with a frown on her face" *Vous n'êtes pas prêt à être servi. Quittez ma présence.* " (You are not ready to be served. Leave my presence" With such rudeness. I was calm and, in my mind, "Delly, you're bigger than this. Just do the needful and fill the form". I didn't have a pen so I had to wait for this "Good Cameroonian" in front of me to finish and hand me his. He did! I filled up with my son already so frustrated and rolling on the floor. You can only imagine the stress I was facing. One eye on him and the other on the form. I managed to fill it up, holding his hand and then queuing again. Two people were in front of me, so I waited for my turn again with Mrs Jezebel. While queuing, I noticed how nice and friendly she was with the people in front of me and secretly wished she would extend that fellowship to me. Then came my second turn. Panicking, I pushed the forms I'd filled and immediately, with a shout (I'm not exaggerating) *"Madame, vous n'avez pas signé ce formulaire. S'il te plaît, je ne veux pas d'un tel désordre"* (Madam, you did not sign this form.

155

Please, I don't want such a disorder). She pushed the forms and it fell down and I silently picked them up. Whispering to myself "Delly, calm down". Don't spoil everything. The fault is yours. You forgot to sign. Again, I had to wait for someone to finish with their pen and I signed. Queued up again. Noticed her demeanour glows whilst with others but the moment she sees me, she immediately goes moody. I know a demon when I see one and I kept telling myself, "Delly, this is a test and you have to pass it in flying colours. Stay calm". Yet again, I gave the forms, this time, everything was correct. She asked for JB's passport and I gave (fingers crossed). Booom! *"Qu'est-ce qui ne va pas. Alors tu n'as pas tamponné le visa de ton fils et tu viens me stresser? Va le tamponner, je n'aime pas le désordre".* (What's wrong. So you didn't stamp your son's visa and you're coming to stress me out? Go stamp, I don't like disorder). And she pushed the passport via the small window... with pain in my heart, heavy eyes, my son crying, I picked it up and turned around. At this point, her other colleagues already noticed she was mean to me as I could see them spying from their respective kiosks. Wow! Delly, you must pass this test. Just go stamp the visa. If you flare up and speak, you might not get your checkout on time and remember, you have a flight to catch to Yaoundé (my Dellycious were waiting at the Airport). I asked around and I was shown where to stamp it. Got into the office and met two women; not knowing what to expect, yet expecting the worst. I was wrong! While one of them was serving another person, the other lady welcomed me and I immediately went "Madam, my son is autistic" please bear with him; before I could complete my sentence, she hushed me and went "I can see. Don't worry, we will do our best. I understand his condition". She said it with a smile. Lord, her words dropped tears from my ears at that stage. She was different. If you're used to Autistic kids, you know how much eye-contact they hate to give. His picture had to be taken and it was such a challenge as he wouldn't look in the Camera. After many failed attempts, this lady kept reassuring me and saying "bother not, let's try one more time". We did (while JB was at his worst behaviour). She managed to get a very blurry picture of him. "This picture is not good but this is the best so far, so we'll manage it". She said, in English with her French

157

accent. She stamped the visa and gave me a pat on my back "Don't worry, I understand the stress. Calm down and all will be fine". Turning to JB (with a smile) she said "Stop stressing you mummy OK? Enjoy your stay in Cameroon". A little calm, I went back to the queue to be served by Mrs Jezebel. Our eyes collided from a distance and I said to myself "Satan, get thee behind me!". It was my turn again and she took everything. Then with a very low tone (still with a frown on her face) she said *"placez vos doigts pour votre empreinte digitale"* (place your fingers for your fingerprints). Imagine the confusion in me "is she talking about my fingerprint or my son's?" I was literally shaking. In confusion, I pulled JB to come close to the fingerprint machine. Oh my! she shouted still with a frown and in French said "your finger prints, not his". At that stage, I'd lost my cool but I kept on. She took all the fingerprints, asked that I hold my son for a snap shot (another stress) and after inputting our details in her computer, she lifted up her head and returned our passports. Still in confusion, I asked, are we done? She obviously ignored me and said in French "Next person". It dawned on me, I had successfully completed my

DIARY OF A SPECIAL MUM

check out routine and it was my turn to speak. I heaved a sigh of relief, held my son, pushed my luggage to the side. The good Cameroonian helping with the luggage had left. He did his best and couldn't continue waiting. Hopefully, someday he stumbles on this and recognizes himself herein as I never got the opportunity to properly say "Thank you!". (My general philosophy is to only speak when my words are better than my silence, otherwise, I will lose my composure and get so loud that I hate myself thereafter). I walked away from the scene and had to complain at least to someone. In those few minutes, I battled with speaking up for myself or speaking to someone to mediate.

Then comes this tall, huge and dark lady in uniform. She seemed calm and willing to hear me speak (from the welcoming look on her face). My eyes were red and heavy, JB pulling my hand for us to go as he noticed I was rather standing to waste more of his time. Autistic kids have their moments; they are such *sweethearts* on a good day and a *handful* on other days. This was obviously not the day for my son and he wasn't having it. "Can I speak with you Mummy?" (English) "Of course, you can!

159

(English words and Accent). "Father Lord, thank you she's Anglophone and I won't stutter with my speaking". (Speaking to myself). My spoken French is horrible, though I understand almost everything. "I have a complaint to make against Madam Jezebel (I gave her complete name) in Kiosk XYZ. She has been so mean to me and I don't know why. Seems you are her colleague and should talk to her because I was silent and didn't express myself but she should never treat another person as such (speaking with teary eyes). From every indication, this particular Jezebel has a reputation of being rude and my complaint didn't seem shocking to the elderly woman. While this Mama is trying to calm me down like "Don't worry, I'll talk to her", Lo and behold, Madam Jezebel had the guts to rudely defend herself from her Kiosk as she'd eavesdropped on our conversation. Lordy Lord, that was when I lost my composure! I abandoned my son at that spot, left the elderly lady and now walked close to Jezebel's Kiosk and at the top of my voice I hushed her! Looking her eyeball-to-eyeball, I rebuked her! I've had enough of you already! Madam, who do you think you are? Are you even a mother? What exactly did I do to you?

What exactly do you consider yourself to be? This life is vanity and none of us is leaving this earth alive! You don't own an ounce of the air you breathe! So calm down and treat people like humans. You can drop dead the next minute! How much of an evil heart can one woman have? Do you want to pretend you didn't notice my son has some medical challenges? Who else do I expect empathy from better than a fellow woman? Do you even have kids? Are you not ashamed of yourself? What did I do to you?

I travelled 12 hours on air to my country and this is what I get from a fellow sister who is rather supposed to be the one to give me water to drink? Guess what? I stuttered while speaking French but she understood every word and was mute. I didn't blink. My words pierced through her heart like an arrow on a mission by a skilled hunter. I saw this "few-minutes-ago-Goliath" suddenly become a frightened kid; shocked to see that same "naive" woman from minutes ago become this supergiant. Like David, I spoke with Authority! Oh, I damned the consequences at that stage and I kept on (her colleagues spying from their respective Kiosks, quite impressed with my guts). What exactly did I do to you? Oh, you know exactly what I'm talking about! You just hated me for no reason. Sister, we are dust! Remember, none of us is leaving here alive and this is all vanity! She had people waiting to be served in front of her but kept her gaze on me. She couldn't ignore the words I unleashed. My son equally went mute while I spoke like "Go Mummy, give it to her". laugh! Then a sudden pat on my back, the elderly lady whispering "it's OK my daughter, calm down now, she has heard you". The calm in my spirit. The entire hall was graveyard-silent as I pulled and pushed my hand luggages towards the exit. I could feel every eye on me as we walked away. I exited and made my way to the luggage area where I was told my main luggage had not arrived. My countenance was quite calm and serene like nothing happened. Of course, nothing had happened. Wink! Fast forward, after my stay in Yaoundé, I had to travel to Douala. I took Cameroon Airlines and when I landed, a thought asked me to go check on Madam Larisa. Yes, she's Larissa and I dare to mention her name now because I'd cast the Jezebel out! *"Nous avons deux Larisas ici, laquelle recherchez-vous?"* (We have two Larissas here, which of them are you looking for?" Her colleague asked. I immediately pointed to her empty Kiosk. Unfortunately, Madam Larissa wasn't on seat. *"À qui dois-je lui dire qui est venu la chercher ? Comment vous appelez-vous madame?"* Her colleague asked. "Just tell her, a special friend of hers stopped by to say hi; the one with the Autistic Son and she will know who I am". I walked away!

All these experiences made outings scary and had me constantly looking over my shoulders. Sadly, 9 out of 10 times, the parent is judged and labelled by onlookers as poor parenting. Over time, I've learnt to be more vigilant and master the triggers that make them act impulsively. If you're keen, you must have noticed, JB or your child will freak out or run away because of a particular need. Be fast and religious about making available that need. Otherwise, they will sort for alternative means of getting it. JB loves potato chips - the cheese and onion flavour is his favourite. I've done all to stop him having them as I learnt it's not quite a good option for his gut. He loves it and will jump on it the minute he sees it. Each time I deprive him of those, JB gets "missing" and you'll end up finding him wherever his crisps can be found. Don't make any assumptions. They are different from regular kids. Their minds function differently and faster. Actually, they don't process information the usual way. While you are thinking, they are acting. While you expect them to see dangers, their minds are on an adventure spree. In their world, there is no harm until they are harmed. They expect the oncoming car to give them a way and not the other way round. They see fire and other harmful objects as toys for experiments. When they set their hearts on something, their minds are on it. You see the road; they see the destination. You see danger, they see adventure. You see embarrassments, they are living their best lives. This should equally point us towards the fact that it is not always about being the perfect parent, nor is it always about our abilities. I am a firm believer in God and I believe in his divine abilities in protecting these kids when we as parents are most vulnerable. Our limitations are evident and, in such moments, we are humbled enough to know we are mere mortals with occasional episodes of errors that could cost us everything. Now you know, other parents were not necessarily careless before losing their kids to nature or social services

TESTIMONIALS

Autism in the African context is still a myth for many. What a bold move for Ms. Delly Singah to come up with a book about this. The focus on her son, Favour, is most vital in reshaping societal perspectives on autism. Favour's story inspires innovation in education, therapy, and technology to accommodate varied learning styles and needs. As a mother at the center of this subject, Delly is pivotal in acting as a major voice / advocate, a caregiver, and an educator to help us understand autism. Her resilience and dedication helps break down stigmas surrounding autism, fostering greater acceptance and inclusivity in communities. Congratulations on this new book.

Prof. Victor W. Mbarika
President Board of Trustees ICT University

"When the winds of life's challenges blow, only those with unwavering determination turn them into a storm of positive change." Delly Singah, as I have known her, is a trailblazer—a fearless advocate in the realm of autism awareness and empowerment. Her journey with her beloved Jesus Boy has not only been a testament to the power of unconditional love but also a clarion call for society to rise to the occasion and address this often-misunderstood condition with empathy and action. This book is more than just a collection of personal reflections; it is a practical manual—one that equips families, caregivers, and communities with the knowledge and inspiration to navigate the

realities of autism. Through her story, Delly opens the door to understanding, fosters hope, and ignites a much-needed conversation in a world where so many are searching for guidance. Diary of a Special Mum is not just a book—it is a movement, a lifeline, and an invaluable tool for anyone seeking to embrace the journey of autism with courage and compassion.

Dr. Richard Munang
Environment & Development Policy Expert

As a medical doctor with over 15 years of experience working with individuals on the autism spectrum, I've learned that autism is as unique as the people it affects.

It is a developmental disorder characterized by differences in social interaction, communication, and behavior patterns, with a wide spectrum of severity, and is diagnosed based on observed behaviors rather than a single lab test; it's considered a neurodiversity, not a disease, meaning there is no "cure" but support can be provided to manage challenges individuals may face due to their autistic traits.

It is imperative for Africans to be educated as such and what better way to get this education across borders - first-hand experience from a Mother's diary whose baby is on the spectrum. I humbly think, this book should be on every shelf across Africa and the world. Again, Autism isn't just a diagnosis—it's a different way of experiencing the world.

Dr. Basile Njei MD, MPH, PhD
Assistant Professor of Medicine.

As a healthcare professional with a background in Nursing and Midwifery practice, understanding and supporting individuals with autism is very crucial. Providing care for individuals with autism requires empathy, adaptability, and patient-centred approaches. Autism is a neurodevelopmental condition that presents challenges with communication, social interaction, and sensory processing. It is essential to create a calm, supportive environment, use clear and effective communication, and adapt care plans to meet each patient's unique needs. Collaborating with families and specialists ensures holistic care, while early intervention and consistent support play a critical role in improving outcomes and enhancing quality of life for individuals with autism.

Loveline Pekeleke
Registered Adult Nurse and Midwife - London

I should be scared. I should restrain him from manipulating my phone. But I was curious. Captured by what seemed like his own curiosity. But Jesus boy moved from one application to the next, playing on a piano I didn't know was in my phone. Trying a melody, I imagined was in his head. Then he moved to the phone camera, wiggling his hand underneath the camera, repeatedly and capturing the movement. I didn't know what to make of it, but I loved that he enjoyed it, that it meant something; it gave some symmetry to a possible disorder around him. We played. I lifted him up, and he giggled heartily and clung to me like a hungry baby clings to his mother's breast. And then when we moved to take

*pictures, he would not stare into the camera. It turned into a game
of monitoring until that second when he would flash a smile, and
we would have something that could remotely capture his stunning
handsomeness. When he strays, we are on alert because his
mother, hawkish, and protective panics. I imagine the routine of
dealing with an autistic kid. How ever-present a parent must be.
How patient and loving. I have done comedy to raise awareness
of autism. But experiencing it made me respect a hands-on autistic
mother. It made me understand her a little more. It made me love
this boy deeply. Every now and then I watch the videos he took
with my phone, and a bright smile comes to me.*

Dr. Kwoh Elonge
Academic Researcher and Comedian - U.S.A

*While being a parent in general is like running a marathon that
never ends, being a parent to a special child is different in that
you do not have the luxury of stops or breaks when you badly need
them. Amidst all the tears, diapers, snort etc, refilling your spirit
and body, and being a lifelong learner are a must so that you can
be the parent your child needs and deserves. With your reserves
for self-care depleted, our collective strength comes in handy. A
listening ear, shared helpful strategies, tools and tips; a shared
conversation/experience with another parent; a community of
like-minded parents; etc. are all the cornerstone of being the best
parent for your child.*

Parenting is a ministry and we are all called to adapt our parenting based on the stage of maturity rather than the age of the child. This is true for ALL parents.

Ivy B Ngwa
Educator, Certified Parent & Mindset Coach. U.K

A multifaceted strategy that tackles societal, educational, and cultural hurdles is needed to empower Africans to comprehend and assist people with special needs. Raising awareness about the nature of disabilities through media campaigns, community outreach, and public discussions can help challenge misconceptions and reduce stigma. This book is a major step in the right direction.

Dr. Valentine Che
Business Lecturer / Technology Consultant United Kingdom

I grew up with little or no knowledge about autism. The first time I got to hear about it seemed to be some sort of taboo or forbidden subject. Many shy away from the subject and would rather not talk about it. Growing up in such an environment made autism a mystery. Fast forward years later, a friend around had a son with special needs. Later, I witnessed JB's step by step growth and how things spiralled. Later on, a close family member had a similar and more challenging case.
I am glad Delly - "A special Mum" mustered courage to share her thrilling, challenging yet rewarding journey with the world. I can't wait to see how this book will inspire and impact many families

169

with the courage to see the unique blessing in parenting a child with special needs. Well done Delly!

Eyong Enoh
Author, Speaker and Football Consultant and Founder of 4pballer

I recognize the crucial need for society to be sensitized regarding autism and other special needs. A significant gap exists in the lack of knowledge of the fundamental aspects of these individuals and their families, which often leads to stigmatization and misunderstanding—due to lack of awareness, leading to societal and cultural misconceptions about their abilities and behaviors. Cultural stigmatisation can manifest in various forms, including social exclusion, negative labeling, and discrimination, which can indirectly impact the mental and emotional well-being of both the child and their family. This societal prejudice not only hampers the development of supportive relationships but also perpetuates isolation for those on the spectrum. Challenging our stereotypes through education and open dialogue is crucial, fostering a culture of acceptance and inclusion that recognizes the unique strengths and contributions of individuals with special needs. "I am continually inspired by the strength and knowledge demonstrated by parents like Delly Singah, who navigate the acceptance complexities of raising children with special needs. Their unique ability is a powerful reminder of the importance of transforming societal perceptions and promoting a more inclusive community."

Silas Akere Tamufor
Senior Quality Assurance Specialist in Research and Development.

As a medical professional and a dedicated mother of a child with autism, I view autism as a spectrum that necessitates a personalized approach in both care and everyday life. From a medical standpoint, it involves early diagnosis and tailored therapies that cater to each child's unique needs, ensuring they can thrive in their own way.

On a personal level, being a parent to a child with autism means navigating various challenges with love, patience, and advocacy. It's about finding joy in the small victories and embracing the journey, knowing that every step forward—no matter how different—represents a significant achievement. Both roles demand deep empathy, resilience, and the belief that every individual with autism possesses immense potential.

That's truly inspiring and uplifting! My journey is a testament to the power of God, persistence, faith, and support. Watching my son outgrow autism and develop into such a calm, intelligent, and loving boy has brought us so much pride and joy. It's clear that the challenges we faced only made our bond stronger and more meaningful. Our experience shows how hope, dedication, and divine support can lead to incredible transformations.

Linda Teyim (aka Linda Brown)
Mental Health Nurse and Registered Child Minder, U.K.

"If they can't learn the way we teach, we teach the way they learn"
[Ole Ivar Lovaas]

DIARY OF A SPECIAL MUM

REFERENCES

American Psychiatric Association. (2013). Diagnostic and statistical manual of mental disorders (5th ed.). Arlington, VA: American Psychiatric Association.

British Dietetic Association (2024) *Autism and Diet, British Dietetic Association (BDA)*. Available at: https://www.bda.uk.com/resource/autism-diet.html (Accessed: 30 January 2025).

Bladder & Bowel UK: Article: The impact of sensory issues on toilet training.

Cooper, K. Loades, M.E., & Russel, A., (2018). Adapting psychological therapies for autism. Research in Autism Spectrum Disorders. 45; 43-50.

Croen, L. A., Zerbo, O., Qian, Y., Massolo, M. L., Rich, S., Sidney, S., & Kripke, C. (2015). The health status of adults on the autism spectrum. Autism, 19(7), 814–823.

Ellison Solicitors (December 2023) Raising kids with additional needs and divorce

Fiene, L., & Brownlow, C. (2015). Investigating interoception and body awareness in adults with and without autism spectrum disorder. Autism Research, 8(6), 709–716.

Garfinkel, S.N., Tiley, C., O'Keeffe, S., Harrison, N.A., Seth, A.K., & Critchley, H.D. (2016). Discrepancies between dimensions of interoception in autism: Implications for emotion and anxiety. Biological Psychology. 114; 117-26.

Karthik Kumar, M. (2021) *What foods should be avoided with autism? 7 foods*, *MedicineNet*. Available at: https://www.medicinenet.com/what_foods_should_be_avoided_with_autism/article.htm (Accessed: 30 January 2025).

Lever, A. G., & Geurts, H. M. (2016). Psychiatric co-occurring symptoms and disorders in young, middle-aged, and older adults with autism spectrum disorder. Journal of Autism and Developmental Disorders, 46(6), 1916–1930.

Maisel, M. E., Stephenson, K. G., South, M., Rodgers, J., Freeston, M. H., & Gaigg, S. B. (2016). Modeling the cognitive mechanisms linking autism symptoms and anxiety in adults. Journal of Abnormal Psychology, 125(5), 692-703.

Roy M., Prox-Vagedes V., Ohlmeier M.D., & Dillo W. (2015). Beyond childhood: psychiatric comorbidities and social background of adults with Asperger syndrome. Psychiatria Danubina, 27(1), 50-59.

Shah, P., Hall, R., Catmur, C., & Bird, G. (2016). Alexithymia, not autism, is associated with impaired interoception. Cortex: A Journal Devoted to the Study of the Nervous System and Behavior, 81, 215-220.

Sizoo, B.B. & Kuiper, E. (2017). Cognitive behavioural therapy and mindfulness-based stress reduction may be equally effective in reducing anxiety and depression in adults with autism spectrum disorders. Research in Developmental Disabilities, 64; 47-55.

South, M. & Rodgers, J. (2017). Sensory, emotional and cognitive contributions to anxiety in autism spectrum disorders. Frontiers in Human Neuroscience, 11: 20.

Spain, D., Sin, J., Chalder, T., Murphy, D., & Happe, F. (2015). Cognitive behavior therapy for adults with autism spectrum disorders and psychiatric co-morbidity: A review. Research in Autism Spectrum Disorders. 9; 151-162.
Udemy (2025) online course: Guide for parenting children with autism and ADHD.

Walters, S., Loades, M. & Russell, A. (2016). A systematic review of effective modifications to cognitive behavioural therapy for young people with autism spectrum disorders. Journal of Autism and Developmental Disorders. 3(2): 137-153.

Weston, L., Hodgekins, J., & Langdon, P.E. (2016). Effectiveness of cognitive behavioural therapy with people who have autistic spectrum disorders: A systematic review and meta-analysis. Clinical Psychology Review. 49, 41-54.

Wheeler, M. (no date) *Tips for women in relationships with partners on the Autism Spectrum, Indiana Resource Center for Autism.* Available at: https://www.iidc.indiana.edu/irca/articles/tips-for-women-in-relationships.html (Accessed: 29 January 2025).

World Health Organization (1993) International classification of mental and behavioral disorders: clinical descriptions and diagnostic guidelines. Mason.

www.ingramcontent.com/pod-product-compliance
Lightning Source LLC
Chambersburg PA
CBHW021540260326
41914CB00001B/100